Maths and Non-verbal Reasoning

Assessment Practice for the CEM test

Ages 8–9 Year 4

Alison Primrose

OXFORD
UNIVERSITY PRESS

Great Clarendon Street, Oxford OX2 6DP

Oxford University Press is a department of the University of Oxford.
It furthers the University's objective of excellence in research, scholarship,
and education by publishing worldwide. Oxford is a registered trade mark
of Oxford University Press in the UK and in certain other countries

Text © Alison Primrose 2023
Illustrations © Oxford University Press 2023

The moral rights of the authors have been asserted

All rights reserved. No part of this publication may be reproduced,
stored in a retrieval system, or transmitted, in any form or by any
means, without the prior permission in writing of Oxford University
Press, or as expressly permitted by law, by licence or under terms
agreed with the appropriate reprographics rights organization.
Enquiries concerning reproduction outside the scope of the above
should be sent to the Rights Department, Oxford University Press,
at the address above.

You must not circulate this work in any other form and you must
impose this same condition on any acquirer

British Library Cataloguing in Publication Data
Data available

978-0-19-277982-3

10 9 8 7 6 5 4 3 2 1

Paper used in the production of this book is a natural, recyclable
product made from wood grown in sustainable forests.
The manufacturing process conforms to the environmental
regulations of the country of origin.

Printed in China

Acknowledgements

Content Development Adviser: Michellejoy Hughes
Content Development Adviser and Reviewer: Jane Cooney
Additional material by Michellejoy Hughes

Page make-up: Integra Software Services
Cover illustrations: Lo Cole
Illustrations: Integra Software Services and Tech-Set Ltd, Gateshead

Although we have made every effort to trace and contact
all copyright holders before publication this has not been
possible in all cases. If notified, the publisher will rectify
any errors or omissions at the earliest opportunity.

Contents

Welcome	4
A Note for Parents	5
How to Use This Book	6

Learning Papers

Number Skills	8
Sequences	12
Number Skills and Pattern Completion	15
Logic and Codes	20
Shape, Space and Grids	24
Position and Direction	29
Measurement and Pairs	36
Statistics and Pattern Recognition	41

Curveball Questions 1:

Logic, Codes and Number Skills	46

Mixed Papers

Mixed Paper 1	48
Mixed Paper 2	53
Mixed Paper 3	59
Mixed Paper 4	65

Curveball Questions 2:

Number Skills, Logic and Sequences	70

Test Papers

Test Paper 1	71
Test Paper 2	80
Keywords	88
11+ Study Guide	90
Answers	A1
Progress Chart	A18

Two further Mixed Papers are available online at www.bond11plus.co.uk

Welcome

The CEM Select Entrance Assessment is a computer-based 11+ test that assesses a child in verbal, non-verbal and mathematical reasoning. It covers English and maths topics that a child will be familiar with from the National Curriculum, but, in common with other 11+ exams, supplements these with verbal reasoning and non-verbal reasoning questions. What makes the CEM exam different from other assessments is the way that it blends English and verbal reasoning in one test and then maths and non-verbal reasoning in another, rather than offering four separate tests. CEM (Centre for Evaluation and Monitoring) do not offer their own practice materials or past papers and deliberately vary the contents of the exam each year, which means that the CEM 11+ is often seen as being more challenging to prepare for.

All Bond 11+ materials are effective preparation for CEM Select and develop the skills and aptitudes that a child needs for success, but CEM-specific titles, like this one, are designed to hone the flexibility of approach essential to overcoming the particular challenges of the CEM test. The Bond system provides learning, information and consolidation so that children have an extended, rich education. Our aim is to familiarise children with the type of questions they will find in the exam and to give them the transferable skills that will allow a child to attempt any question in any exam.

Bond offers a complete, flexible programme of preparation materials that you can adapt to your child's specific needs and to the requirements of the exam, or exams. There are timings provided for each section. Children can complete a paper in one sitting, using the overall timings, or in smaller sections. The CEM online exam has an additional 25% time allowance for candidates needing additional support. If this applies to your child, add an extra 25% for each timed section.

Why Use a Book to Prepare for an Online Test?

Since 2022, the CEM Select 11+ test has only been offered as a computer-based assessment. Whilst it is worth spending some test-practice time using an online platform such as Bond Online to gain familiarity with completing assessments through a digital interface, books remain a highly effective way of developing the skills necessary for success in a structured way whilst reducing screen time.

Not Just for the CEM Select 11+

This book has been designed to be especially effective preparation for the rigours of the CEM 11+ test, but the skills can be applied to any 11+ exams or independent school entrance exams and are also great for engaged pupils looking for an extra challenge or to ready themselves for secondary school.

Remember to keep checking in with your school of choice so that you know which exam they use – schools do change their exam boards from time to time. If your exam board does change, all is not lost. This book will still have been good preparation for other exam boards.

KEY STUDY SKILLS

Working towards an entrance exam can be an exciting challenge. It is the chance to learn new things and to prepare for secondary school. Here are some tips to help you:

- Create a study schedule so that you have a regular routine.
- Balance short bursts of practice with longer assessment papers.
- Create a quiet study space with pencils, an eraser, paper for working out, your books and a notebook for copying strategies in. If you study in different places, keep everything in a box that you can take with you.
- Write down strategies to solve new topics, but don't forget to revise and consolidate.
- Limit distractions such as television, technology and games when you are studying.
- Remember that errors are useful. They are part of the journey to success.

A Note for Parents

Parents have a crucial role in helping children and motivating them. Here are some ways that you can really make a difference.

- Check your child is working at the right level. The goal is being able to score 85% on average. It's demotivating if they can't complete questions. It is also important that they work through the system so that they are at the right level for the exam at the right time.
- Mark work promptly and go through errors. If papers have not been marked, a child has no idea how they are doing or whether they are repeating the same mistake.
- Use the Bond Handbooks to help your child understand new techniques.
- Limit the range of homework you give your child. The best results are achieved by a system that gradually increases in difficulty. Completing lots of books and papers doesn't guarantee your child's success and often creates stress.
- If your child is struggling with something specific, add additional support in that area. If your child is not achieving an 85% average in CEM-specific books you can also use other subject-specific Bond Assessment Practice books at the same level or Bond 10 Minute Tests for consolidation.
- Communication is key. Remain positive and encourage your child to focus on the positive. No exam is going to ask for 100% so pushing for that is unrealistic and stressful.
- If your child is constantly struggling, be realistic over whether a selective education is the right choice for your child now. Many children move to a selective school for their GCSEs or A levels so not going to a selective school now doesn't mean they never will. It is about finding the best school for your child.

How to Use This Book

This book includes many step-by-step techniques for solving different question types. If further support is needed it can be used alongside one or more of the Bond Handbooks, which offer insights into the full range of questions that might occur in the exam.

- The first section of the book is the Learning Papers that focus on key skills with worked examples then lots of questions for consolidation.
- The second section of the book is Mixed Papers so that children continue to consolidate and do not forget what they have learnt. Go online at **www.bond11plus.co.uk** and register for free resources to get two additional Mixed Papers.
- The final section includes two full Test Papers, which can be broken down into shorter sections for more focussed practice, or can be used as full mock tests for that all-important exam practice.
- There is an 11+ study guide at the back of the book with some useful hints and tips.
- There are fully worked out answers to explain how an answer has been reached.

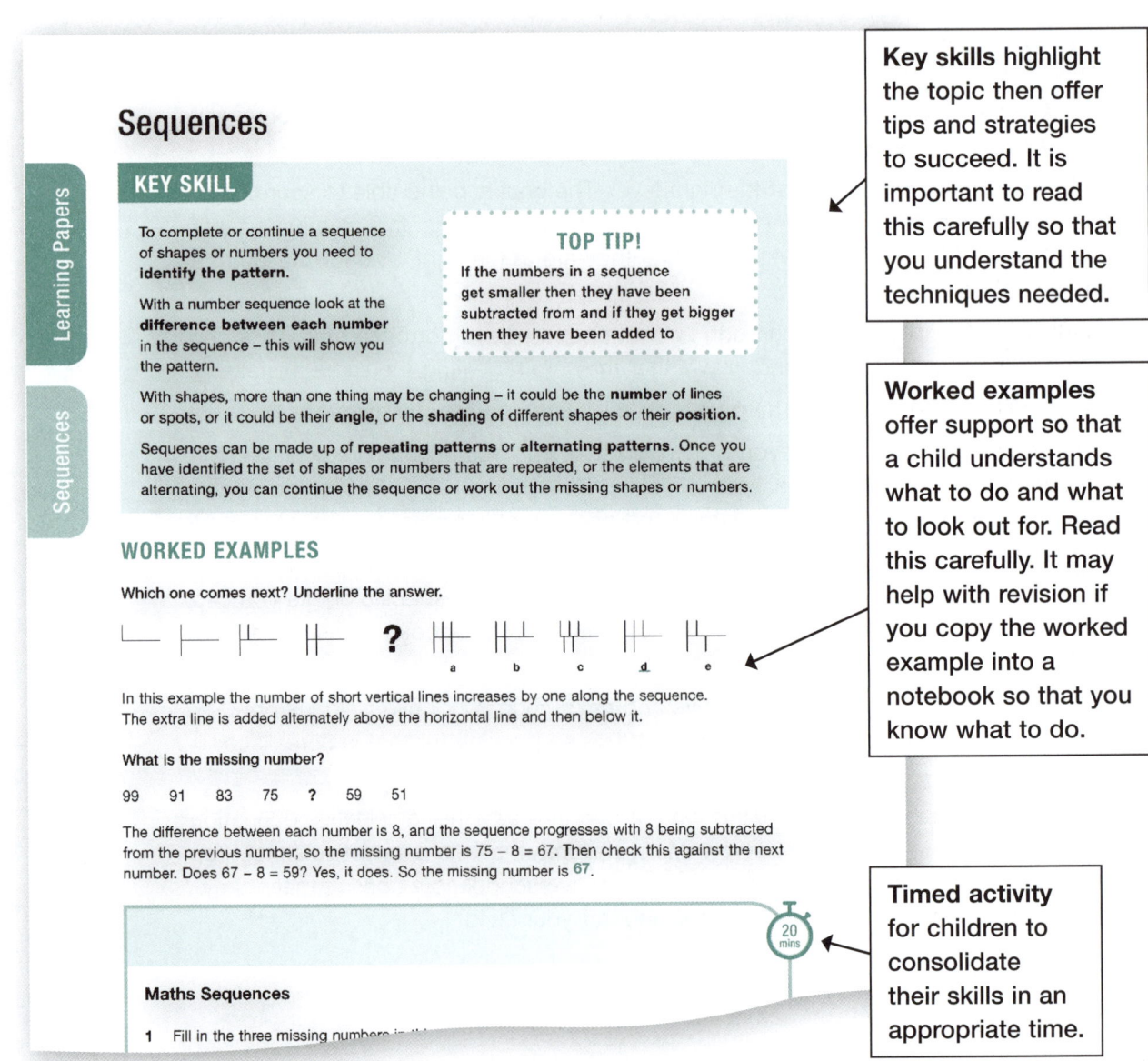

Key skills highlight the topic then offer tips and strategies to succeed. It is important to read this carefully so that you understand the techniques needed.

Worked examples offer support so that a child understands what to do and what to look out for. Read this carefully. It may help with revision if you copy the worked example into a notebook so that you know what to do.

Timed activity for children to consolidate their skills in an appropriate time.

KEY MATHS AND NON-VERBAL REASONING SKILLS

The Bond Maths and Non-Verbal Reasoning Book covers the elements that are found in the CEM online 11+ exam, but is useful for all CEM-style online and written 11+ exams. The Learning Papers cover the following key skills:

- **Mathematics** – a wide range of topics including data, arithmetic and problem solving
- **NVR** – including rotational, reflection, series, sequences and similarities
- **Spatial** – including cubes/nets, 2D and 3D shapes, transformations, and shape combinations.

The Mixed Papers ensure the key skills are consolidated thoroughly then the Test Papers give children the opportunity to get used to the exam process as a natural progression of each book. Don't forget that a rounded education is key. Get used to reading graphs, timetables and charts. Try doing Sudoku and number games, play online games like Tetris or Snake and have a go at some logic and number puzzles – Bond has a number of puzzle books to help make this more fun. Create an ongoing list of strategies or techniques such as 'how to find volume' or 'how to multiply with decimals' to extend your maths skills.

Each book is part of the Bond system with books increasing gradually in difficulty. Once your child has completed this book, there is a clear progression in starting the next book level if your child has an average of 85% in this book. If they have achieved an average of 70% – 85%, then another book at the same level as this one will provide further support. If your child has achieved less than a 70% average, then moving down a level will be most useful. Once your child has developed the skills needed at a lower level, they can move up with confidence.

Learning Papers

Number Skills

KEY SKILL

Remember:

- These words indicate addition – **total**, add, sum, altogether, increase.
- These words indicate subtraction – take away, minus, **difference**, less than, more than, decrease.

Look out for these words in written problems as they indicate what sort of calculation you need to do.

Keep practising your times tables! Multiplication and division are inverse processes – that means they are the opposite of each other. Being confident with your times tables makes multiplication and division calculations much easier. When a number can be divided exactly by another number it is a **multiple** of that number. Times tables give you multiples. A factor is a number that can divide exactly into another number with no remainder, e.g. 3 is a **factor** of 9. A product is the answer you get when two or more numbers are multiplied together. For example, the product of 2 and 3 is 6 as 2 x 3 = 6.

Rounding

To **round** a number to the nearest ten look at the digit in the units column. If it is 5 or more, then the number in the tens column increases by one. If it is less than 5 it stays the same. If you are rounding to the nearest hundred, look at the number in the tens column and if it is 5 or more increase the hundreds by one. So when you are rounding to any given number, always look at the digits in the column to the right to see if the number should increase by one or not.

WORKED EXAMPLES

Rounding to the nearest 10 – so look at the units column:

5<u>7</u>   7 is more than 5, so the number rounded to the nearest 10 is **60**

5<u>3</u>   3 is less than 5, so the number rounded to the nearest 10 is **50**

Identifying the correct calculation

What number is 15 <u>less than</u> 33?   Less than indicates subtraction, so 33 − 15 = **18**

What is the <u>sum</u> of 12 and 72?   Sum of indicates addition, so 12 + 72 = **84**

What is the <u>difference</u> between 100 and 67?   Difference indicates subtraction, so 100 − 67 = **33**

Multiplication

Example: If you know that 4 × 7 = 28, then you also know that:

28 ÷ 4 = 7   28 ÷ 7 = 4   28 is a multiple of 4   28 is a multiple of 7

Place Value

1 Round these numbers to the nearest 100:

  a 466 .... **b** 239 ....

  c 2990 .... **d** 3581 ....

2 Round these numbers to the nearest 1000:

  a 3752 .... **b** 9549 ....

  c 150 .... **d** 1959 ....

> **TOP TIP!**
> To round to the nearest thousand you need to inspect the digit in the hundreds column

Addition and Subtraction

3 1000 − 325 = 600 + ...

> **TOP TIP!**
> Keep the decimal point in line vertically when doing calculations with money that involve both pounds and pence

4 Nehmat has £30. She buys a dress for £19 and a top for £8.50. How much money does she have left? ....

5 Ravi has three letters to post. The postage stamps for these will cost 49p for one letter, 82p for the second letter and £1.25 for the third letter.

  a How much money does he need altogether? ....

  b How much change will he get from a £10 note? ....

6 Marco is given a £25 gift card for his birthday. He goes to buy some books. Some cost £3.50 and others are £4.99.

  a If he buys four books at £3.50, how much money will he have left on the gift card? ....

b Using the money left on his gift card, how many of the £4.99 books can he buy?

....

7 Lionel adds 13 red marbles to his collection of blue and white marbles. He now has 66 marbles in **total**.

a How many marbles were in the jar before adding in the red ones? ....

Of the new total, half are blue and the rest are white or red.

b How many marbles are blue? ....

> **total** The sum of a number of values all added together

c How many are white? ....

8 Complete the missing numbers and symbols in this grid so that the sums going across and the sums going down are correct.

13	+	**a**	=	15
−		+		−
b	**c**	1	=	**d**
=		=		=
6	+	**e**	=	**f**

a ....

b ....

c ....

d ....

e ....

f ....

Multiplication and Division

9 4 × 3 × 10 = ...

10 Share £360 equally between 9 people.

....

11 30 × 50 = ... ÷ 2

> **TOP TIP!**
>
> To complete division more easily, use the short division method: 3 does not go into 1, so write a zero above it and carry the 1 over to the next column to create the number 10. Then 3 goes into 10 three times, with a remainder of 1. Write 3 above the 10 and carry over the 1 to create the number 15. Then 3 goes into 15 five times, so write 5 above it
>
> ```
>     0  3  5
>   3|1 ¹0 ¹5
> ```

12 Underline the numbers that are **multiples** of 3:

360   471   23   35   150   41   81

Combination Operations

13 There are 240 children in a school and 8 classes, which are all the same size.

   a How many children are there in each class? ....

   The children are divided into four house teams. The red and blue teams have 62 members each and the green team has 57 members.

   b How many children are there in the fourth yellow team? ....

14 A variety box of 24 ice creams has 6 chocolate, 6 vanilla and 6 strawberry. The rest are mango flavour.

   a How many mango ice creams are there in the box? ....

   b How many chocolate ice creams would there be in five variety boxes? ....

   c What fraction of each box is made up of vanilla ice creams? ....

15 Natalie's jam recipe uses twice as much sugar as raspberries. Natalie uses 3 kg of raspberries to make some jam. The recipe says to add 500 ml of water for each kg of raspberries. Each kg of sugar will produce two jars of jam.

   a What weight of sugar does Natalie need? ....

   b How much water does Natalie have to add? ....

   c How many jars of jam will this mixture make? ....

> **TOP TIP!**
> To complete multiplication more easily, use the written column method. Make sure you work from right to left and add on any numbers you carry over. For example, 4 x 3 = 12, so the 2 is placed below the 3 and the 1 is carried over in this calculation. The 1 is added on to the next answer: 1 x 3 = 3 and 3 + 1 = 4
>
> ```
>     1 4
>   ×   3
>   ─────
>     4 2
>     1
> ```

Sequences

KEY SKILL

To complete or continue a sequence of shapes or numbers you need to **identify the pattern**.

With a number sequence look at the **difference between each number** in the sequence – this will show you the pattern.

> **TOP TIP!**
> If the numbers in a sequence get smaller then they have been subtracted from and if they get bigger then they have been added to

With shapes, more than one thing may be changing – it could be the **number** of lines or spots, or it could be their **angle**, or the **shading** of different shapes or their **position**.

Sequences can be made up of **repeating patterns** or **alternating patterns**. Once you have identified the set of shapes or numbers that are repeated, or the elements that are alternating, you can continue the sequence or work out the missing shapes or numbers.

WORKED EXAMPLES

Which one comes next? Underline the answer.

In this example the number of short vertical lines increases by one along the sequence. The extra line is added alternately above the horizontal line and then below it.

What is the missing number?

99   91   83   75   **?**   59   51

The difference between each number is 8, and the sequence progresses with 8 being subtracted from the previous number, so the missing number is 75 – 8 = 67. Then check this against the next number. Does 67 – 8 = 59? Yes, it does. So the missing number is **67**.

Maths Sequences

1 Fill in the three missing numbers in this number chain.

42 → ÷3 → ◯ → +30 → ◯ → ×2 → ◯

2 What number comes next? 46, 38, 30, 22, ...

3 What are the missing numbers in each of these number pattern chains?

    a 12, 16, 20, 24, ..., ...

    b 64, 56, 48, ..., ...

    c 319, 309, ..., 289, 279, ...

    d 76, 71, ..., 61, ..., 51

4 What number comes next in this sequence? 104, 109, 114, 119, ...

5 This machine adds 10, then divides by 2. What numbers have gone into it?

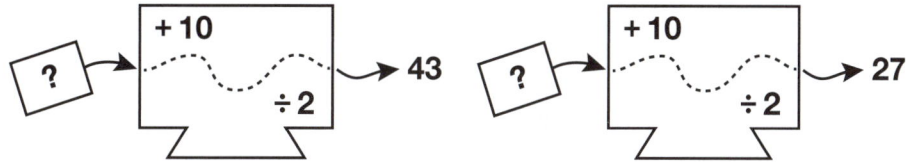

    a ....   **b** ....

NVR Sequences

Which one comes next?
Underline the answer.

> **TOP TIP!**
> Remember more than one thing might be changing along the sequence

6
                                                      a   b   c   d   e

7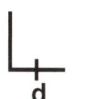
                                                      a   b   c   d   e

8
                                                      a   b   c   d   e

9
                                                      a   b   c   d   e

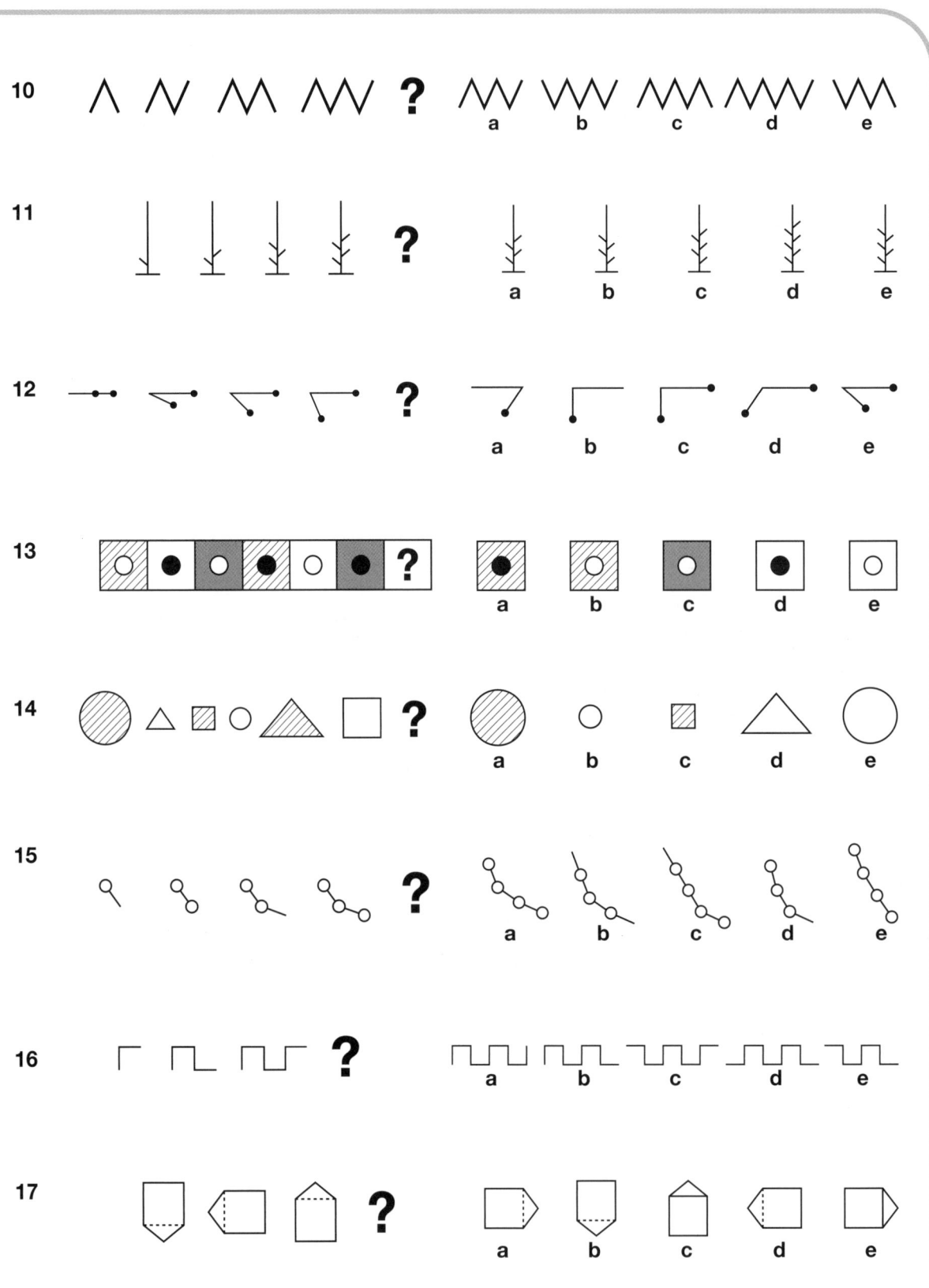

Number Skills and Pattern Completion

> ### KEY SKILL
>
> A whole number or shape can be divided into parts.
>
> For example, tenths have ten equal parts and can be shown as decimals where one-tenth is 0.1, or as a fraction $\frac{1}{10}$.
>
> The next column to the right in a decimal number is the hundredths. That is when a whole number has been divided equally into 100 parts, so one-hundredth is 0.01 or $\frac{1}{100}$.
>
> Common fractions are a half $\frac{1}{2}$, a quarter $\frac{1}{4}$ and three quarters $\frac{3}{4}$. But a whole can be divided into any number of equal parts and that number goes at the bottom of the fraction. The top number in a fraction is called the numerator. The bottom number in a fraction is called the denominator.
>
> To simplify a fraction, find a number that can divide exactly into both numbers. For example, in the fraction $\frac{5}{25}$ both numbers can be divided by 5: $5 \div 5 = 1$ and $25 \div 5 = 5$
>
> Therefore $\frac{5}{25}$ can be simplified to $\frac{1}{5}$
>
> When adding fractions, make sure the denominators are the same, and then add the numerators.
>
> To find a fraction of an amount the amount has to be divided by the number at the bottom of the fraction – so you divide by 2 to find $\frac{1}{2}$, or you divide by 4 to find $\frac{1}{4}$, and so on.

WORKED EXAMPLES

Sixty stamps are shared equally between four children. What fraction do they each get?

The amount is to be shared into 4 equal parts so each part is one-quarter or $\frac{1}{4}$.

How many stamps do they get each? $\frac{1}{4}$ of 60 is $60 \div 4 =$ **15**

Which shape or pattern on the right belongs to the group on the left?
Underline the answer.

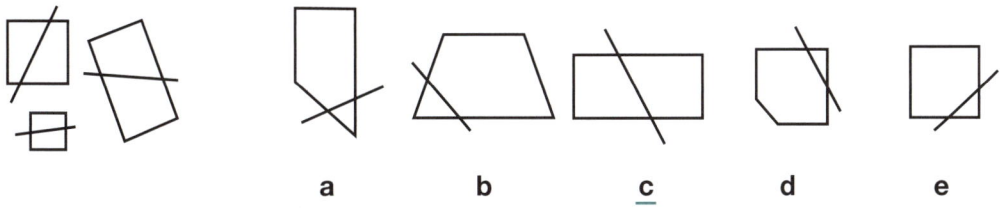

a   b   c   d   e

The shapes on the left are all similar – they are all rectangles and they all have a straight line crossing them from one side to the opposite side.

Fractions

1 There are 80 sweets in a bag. One-quarter are orange, 20 are lemon, 10 are blackberry and the rest are apple.

    a How many apple-flavoured sweets are there? ....

    b What proportion of the whole bag is made up of orange and lemon sweets? .....

    c If each flavour is shared equally between ten friends, how many of each flavour does each friend get?

    orange ....   lemon ....

    blackberry ....   apple ....

2 What number comes next? $4\frac{1}{2}$, 6, $7\frac{1}{2}$, 9 ....

3 Draw a line between each fraction and its correct diagram. The first one has been done for you.

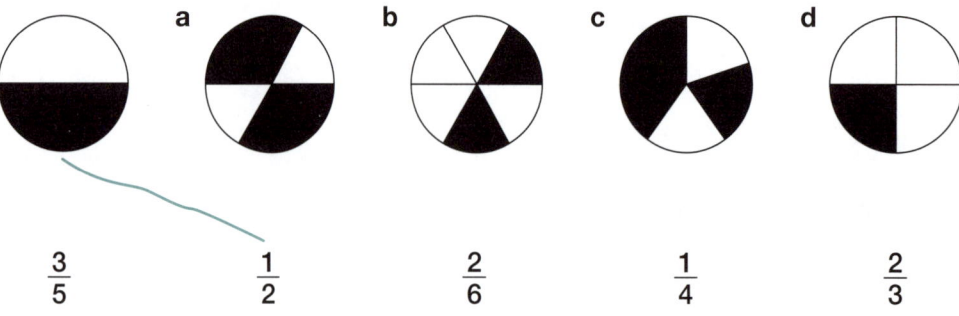

4 Shade in the fraction of each shape.

Example:

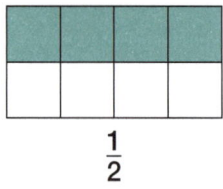

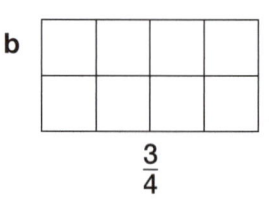

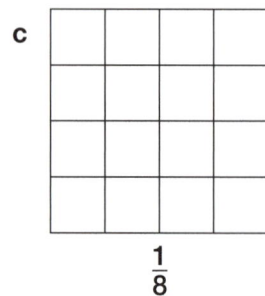

5 Fill in the boxes to complete these fractions.

a $\dfrac{3}{\square} = \dfrac{2}{4} = \dfrac{\square}{8}$
b $\dfrac{2}{10} = \dfrac{\square}{100} = \dfrac{1}{\square}$
c $\dfrac{6}{8} = \dfrac{3}{\square} = \dfrac{\square}{40}$

6 Draw a line between the numbers that have the same value.

$\dfrac{1}{2}$ $\dfrac{75}{100}$

$\dfrac{3}{4}$ 0.7

$\dfrac{7}{10}$ 0.25

$\dfrac{1}{4}$ $\dfrac{6}{12}$

> **TOP TIP!**
>
> The first two digits after a decimal point can be written as a fraction over 100. For example, 0.50 is $\dfrac{50}{100}$ and this can be simplified to $\dfrac{1}{2}$.
>
> Don't forget 0.5 is the same as 0.50, 0.2 is the same as 0.20, and so on!

Decimals

7 Write the following decimal numbers in digits.

  a Four hundred and two and four hundredths ....

  b Seven hundred and two thousand, seventy-two and seven tenths ....

8 Order these numbers from smallest to largest.

  0.1   100   10.1   10.01   100.1   0.01

  .... < .... < .... < .... < .... < ....

> **TOP TIP!**
>
> Write the numbers in a vertical list [or in a grid], making sure the decimal points are in line with one another. Look for the lowest numbers before the decimal points, then look at the next column to find the smallest and so on

9 Fill in the missing number.

  1.42 × .... = 142

10 Write these decimal numbers in order of size.

  4.59   5.01   4.84   5.10   4.58

  .... < .... < .... < .... < ....

NVR Similarities

Which shape or pattern on the right belongs to the group on the left?

Underline the answer.

TOP TIP!
Remember to check all of the answer options given to make sure that you have selected the best answer

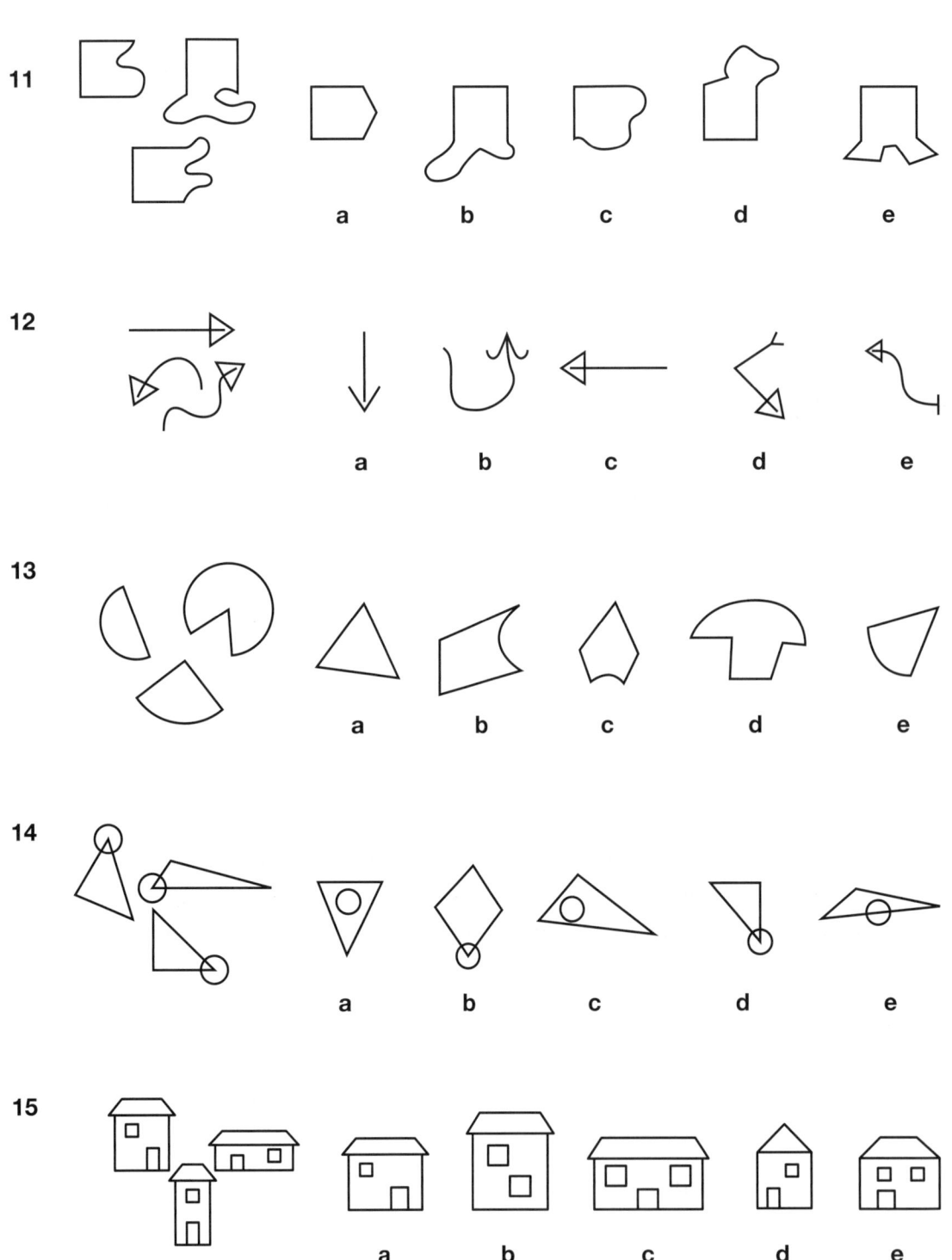

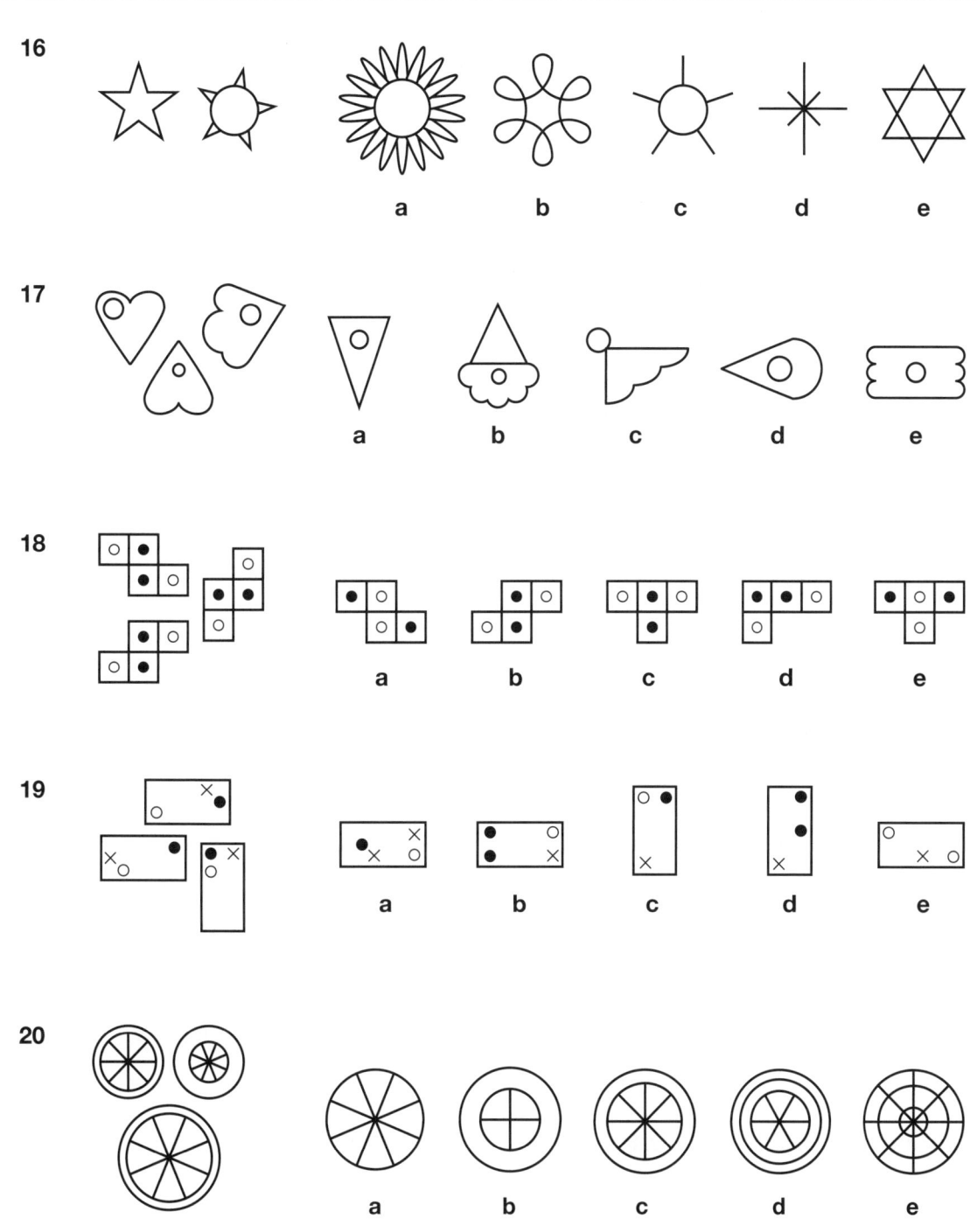

Logic and Codes

KEY SKILL

For written logic problems it can be helpful to draw a diagram showing the information that has been given in the question.

In questions where the information that you need is given in a table, remember to look carefully at the labels for each column of data and follow the columns and rows accurately when reading off the information. It may help to use a ruler to do this.
In NVR Code questions, find two shapes that have the same first letter and look for what they have in common. (This could be the shape, size, pattern, and so on.) Use this to help find the first letter of the shape or pattern you have been given. Then do the same to find the second letter.

WORKED EXAMPLE

Which code matches the shape or pattern given at the end of each line? Underline the answer.

Find two shapes that have the same first letter and look for what they have in common.
The first letter of these codes refers to the shape (A is a circle, B is a triangle, C is a square).
The second letter refers to the shading (X has diagonal lines, Y is black).

NVR Codes

Which code matches the shape or pattern given at the end of each line?
Underline the answer.

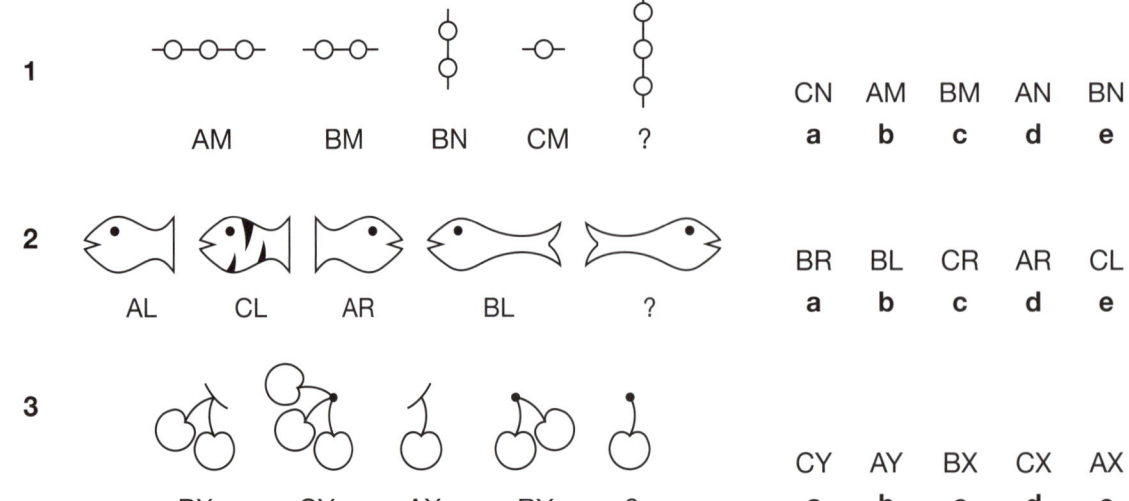

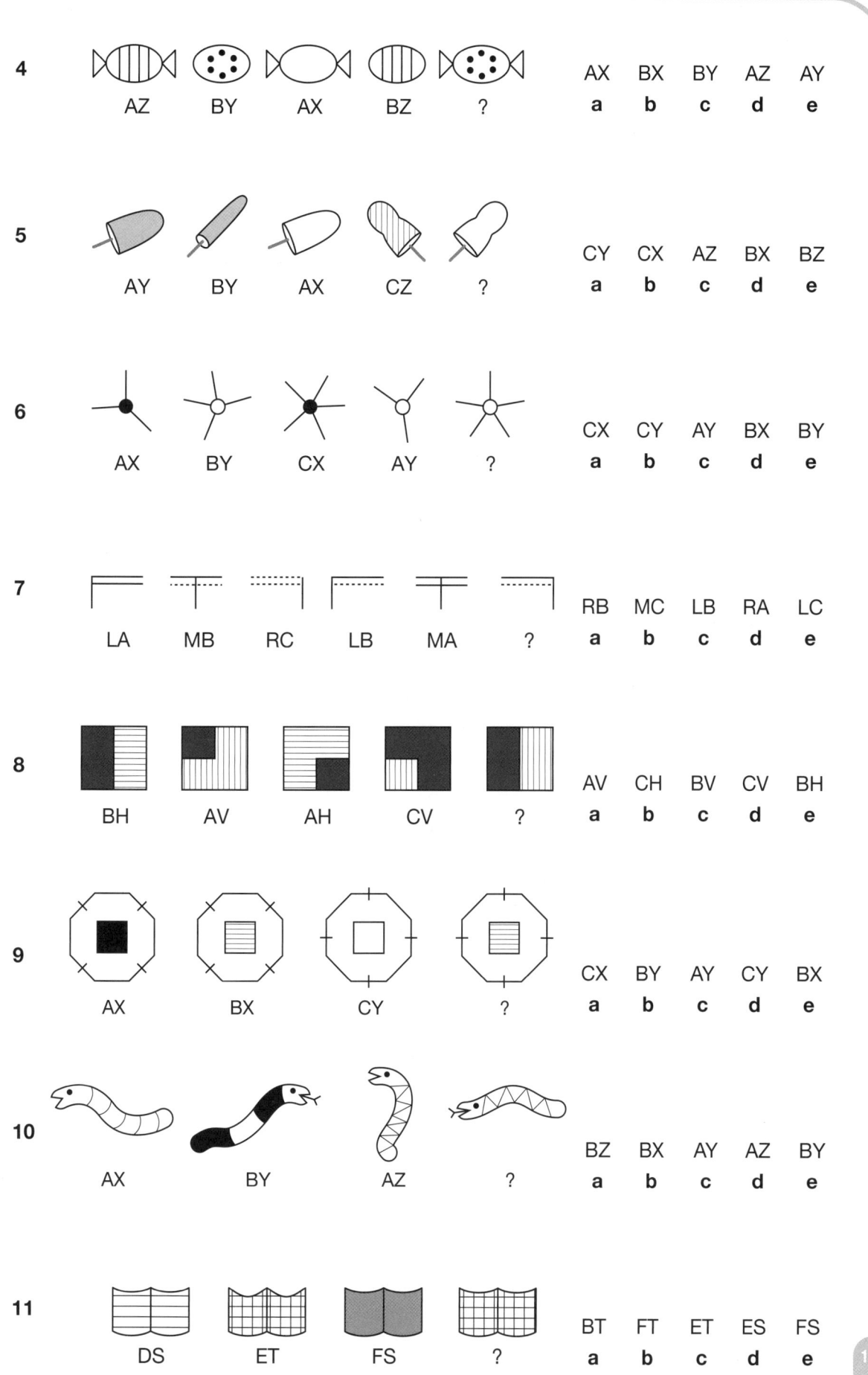

Word and Logic Problems

12 A candle burns at 1 cm per hour. The candle is 12 cm tall when it is lit at 3.30 p.m.

> **TOP TIP!**
> If you find a word problem tricky remember drawing a diagram with the information given can help

    a How tall will the candle be at 5.30 p.m.?

    ....

    b How long will it take to burn 5 cm of the candle?

    ....

    c What time will it be when the candle is 6 cm tall? ....

13 Asim, Tom and Hani took the top three places in a competition. Asim was not first. Tom was not third. Hani did better than Tom.

    Who was in second place? ....

14 Amal is younger than Tim. Tim is older than Sol. Ben is younger than Amal and Sol.

    Who is the eldest of the four boys? ....

15 Look carefully at this table and then answer the questions that follow.

	Likes dogs		**Does not like dogs**	
Likes cats	Julie		Taya	
Does not like cats	Ted		Ray	

    a Who likes cats but not dogs? ....

    b Who likes cats and dogs? ....

    c Add these children's names to the table in the correct places:

    Ben – likes cats but not dogs   Asher – does not like cats or dogs

    Bill – likes dogs but not cats   Aman – likes cats and dogs

16 Tom has a times tables test every day with marks out of ten. On the first day one week he gets seven out of ten, and on the second day he gets nine out of ten. His total number of marks after five days is 46.
How many marks out of ten did he get on the last day?

....

2

17 The chart below shows the number of pairs of different types of socks that pass through a boarding school laundry each week for a group of boys.

	Sun	**Mon**	**Tue**	**Wed**	**Thur**	**Fri**	**Sat**
Grey		20	20	20	20	20	20
Sports	12	15	20	20	10	10	20
Coloured	20	2	4	3	3	20	20

a Each boy wears a clean pair of grey socks each weekday.
How many boys are in the group?

....

b If each boy wears a clean pair of sports socks for any games sessions, on which days do all the boys have a games session?

....

2

18 There are 12 steps in a staircase. Each step is 10 cm high.

a How high is the top of the staircase?

....

b Ashwin goes up eight steps, then back down five steps and stays there.
How many centimetres above the ground level is he now?

....

c If James stays on the seventh step, what is the difference in height between his feet and the step on which Ashwin is standing?

....

3

Total 28

Logic and Codes

Shape, Space and Grids

KEY SKILL

It is important to learn the names of common 2D and 3D shapes. If you are not sure about any of these look them up in the glossary at the end of the book.

2D shapes:

- Quadrilateral, square, rectangle, trapezium, kite, parallelogram
- Triangle, equilateral, right angle triangle, isosceles, scalene
- Circle, semicircle
- Pentagon, hexagon, octagon.

3D shapes (or solids):

- Cube, cuboid, cylinder, prism, pyramid, sphere.

Solid shapes have edges, vertices and faces; and the edges and faces may be flat or curved.

- When a shape is reflected in a mirror, the mirror line is called the line of symmetry. When identifying lines of symmetry in shapes imagine folding the shape over – the two halves should cover each other. Patterns in grids are often symmetrical with grid lines providing lines of symmetry.

Compass points can be used to give directions and angles:

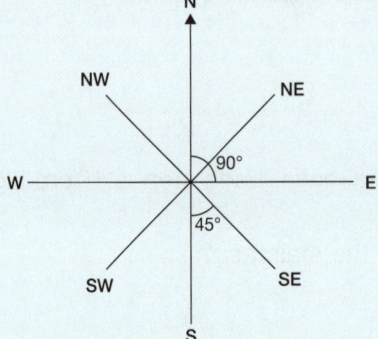

WORKED EXAMPLE

Which pattern completes the larger shape or grid? Underline the answer.

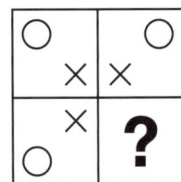 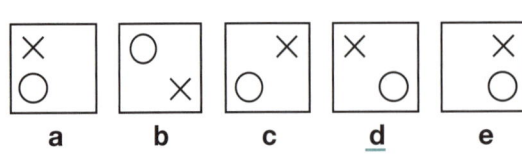

In this example the grid lines are lines of symmetry. Imagine folding the top half of the grid over the lower half – it will give you an X in the top left corner of the empty square and a circle in the lower right corner of that square. You can check this by holding a mirror along the horizontal grid line.

Shape

1. How many flat faces are there on a cylinder and what shape are they? ....

2. Complete this table describing 2D shapes.

Shape	Number of angles	Must it have right angles?	Number of sides
Rectangle			
Octagon			
Triangle			
Hexagon			

3. Draw a quadrilateral with one right angle.

> **REMEMBER!**
> A right angle = 90°
> An acute angle is less than 90°
> An obtuse angle is larger than 90° and less than 180°

4. Put a tick inside the angles drawn below that are acute angles.

    a   b   c   d

5. Complete this sentence by adding in the missing numbers.

A cube has .... square faces, ... straight edges and

.... vertices (or corners).

NVR Grids

Which pattern completes the larger shape or grid? Underline the answer.

6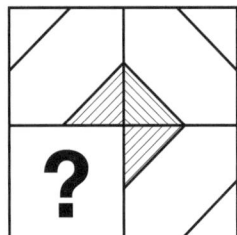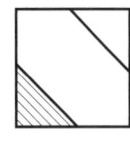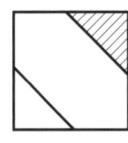
                                                             a   b   c   d   e

7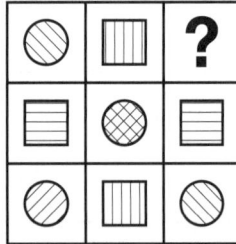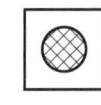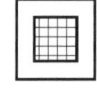
                                                             a   b   c   d   e

8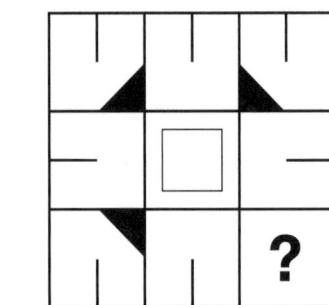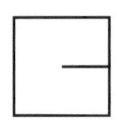
                                                             a   b   c   d   e

9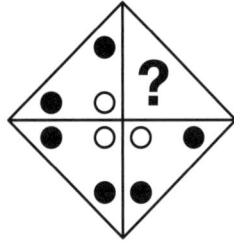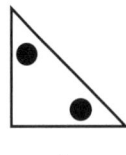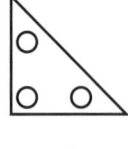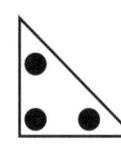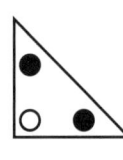
                                                             a   b   c   d   e

10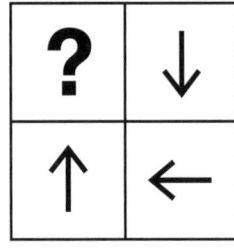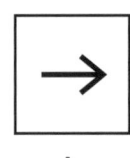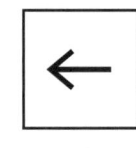
                                                             a   b   c   d   e

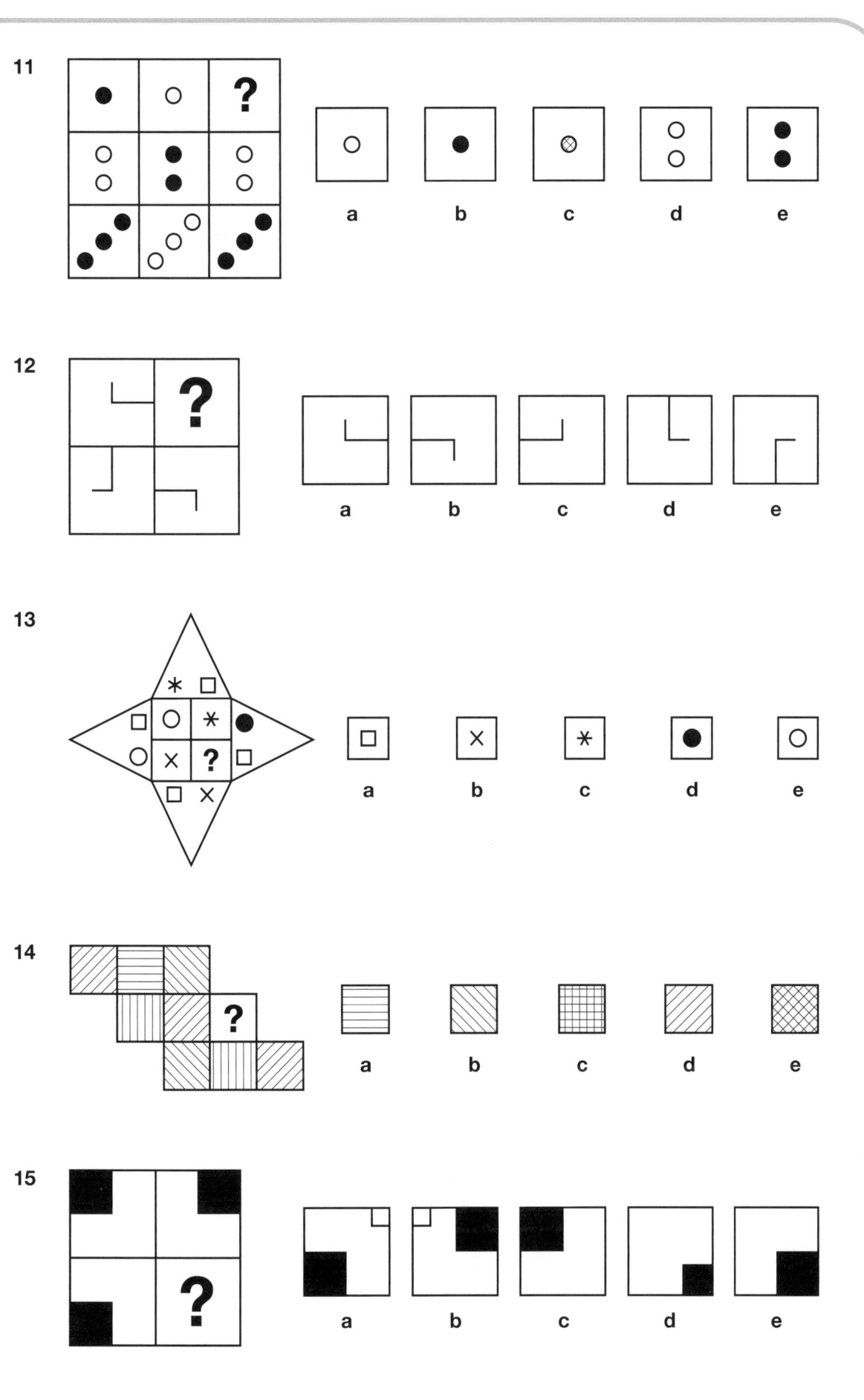

16

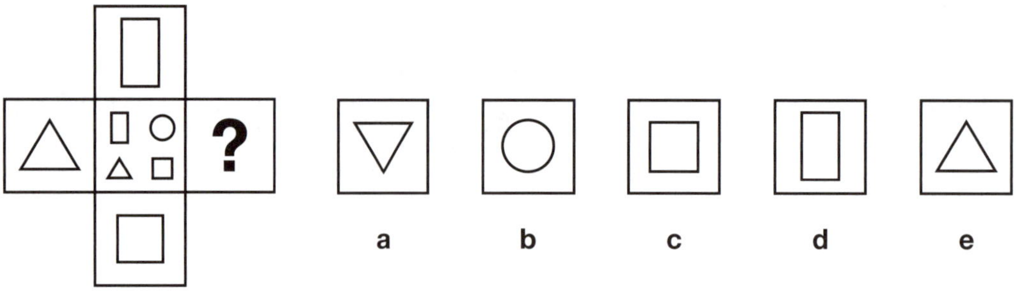

a b c d e

Angles and Direction

17 Connor is standing facing north. He turns 90 degrees in an anticlockwise direction. Which direction is he now facing? ....

18 Through how many degrees does the minute hand of a clock rotate when it goes from half past three to four o'clock? ....

19 A pizza is divided into five equal pieces. What is the angle of each slice?

....

20 A spinner rotates $1\frac{1}{2}$ times before stopping. Through how many degrees does it spin? ....

21 How many degrees make up three right angles? ....

22 A ship is sailing in a north-easterly direction. It turns clockwise through 135 degrees. Which direction is it now travelling? ....

23 How many right angles are there in 360 degrees? ....

24 A car goes along a straight road from east to west, ending at a T junction. It turns left at the T junction then left again. All of the junctions are right angles. Which direction is it now travelling? ....

Total 27

Position and Direction

KEY SKILL

Translation describes the movement of a 2D shape across a grid. The description gives the number of squares that each point moves, firstly in a horizontal direction (right or left) and secondly in a vertical direction (up or down).

Compass points can be used to describe angle, position or direction (see page 24).

Reflections are symmetrical images, where the mirror line or line of reflection is a line of symmetry.

WORKED EXAMPLE

Symmetry. Which pattern on the right is a reflection of the pattern on the left? Underline the answer.

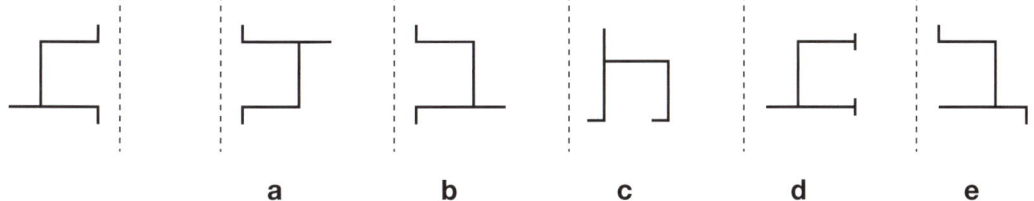

a   <u>b</u>   c   d   e

Coordinates

1.

TOP TIP!

Coordinates always give the number along the *x* or horizontal axis first, followed by the number from the *y* or vertical axis. 'Along the hall and up the stairs' can be an easy way to help you remember the order!

What are the coordinates for the points A, B and C?

A .... B .... C ....

2

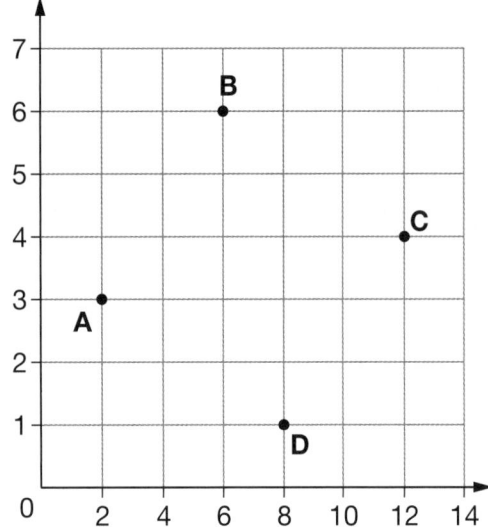

What are the coordinates for the points A, B, C and D?

A .... B ....

C .... D ....

3

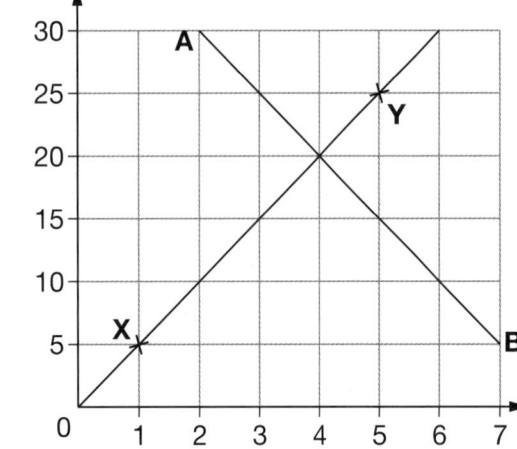

a What are the coordinates of the points X and Y?

X .... Y ....

b What are the coordinates for the point where the line AB crosses the line XY?

....

4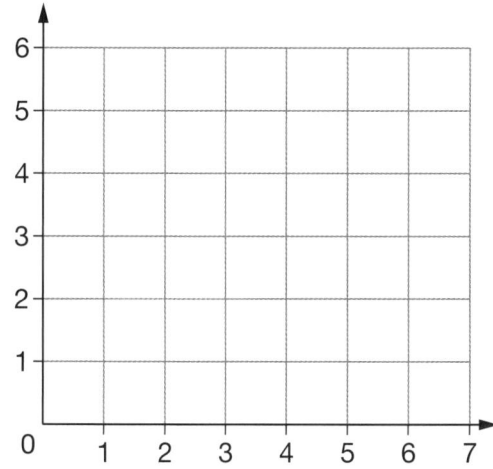

Plot the following points on the grid above.
Join them in the order they are given, and join point E to point A.

A (1,1)   **B** (5,1)   **C** (6, 3)   **D** (5,6)   **E** (1,4)

What is the name of the polygon you have drawn?   ....

5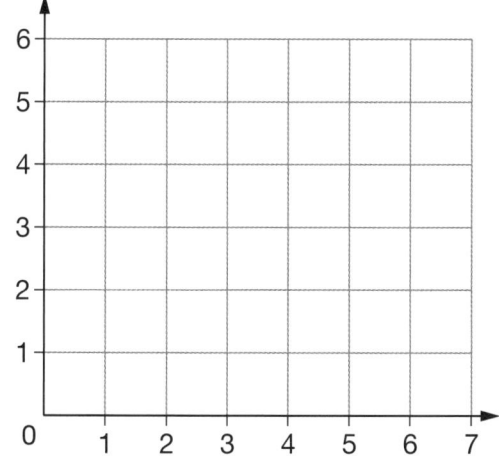

Draw two straight lines on the grid above, one from
the point (0,0) to (6,6), the second line from (1,3) to (4,0).
What are the coordinates of the point where the two lines cross?   ....

6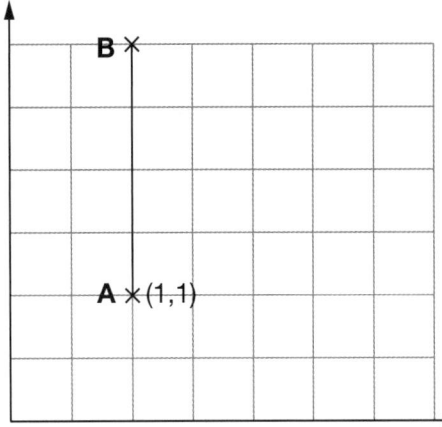

The axes here are not numbered. If the coordinates of point A are (1,1) what are the coordinates of point B if the same scale (numbering) is used on both axes?

....

7   If a horizontal line is drawn on a graph going through the point (3,4), which of the following points will be on the line? Underline them.

(1,3)   (1,4)   (3,3)   (4,3)   (4,4)   (3,5)   (5,4)   (5,6)

8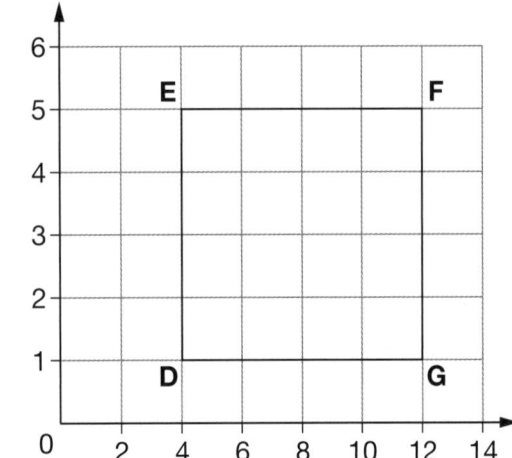

What are the coordinates of the point at the centre of the square DEFG?

....

Transformations

9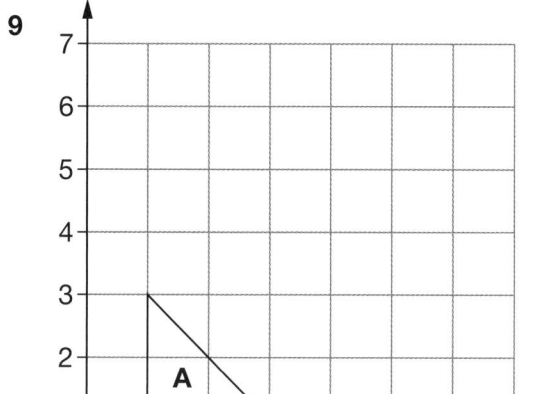

Draw the new position of shape A when it is translated (moved) right 4 and up 3.

10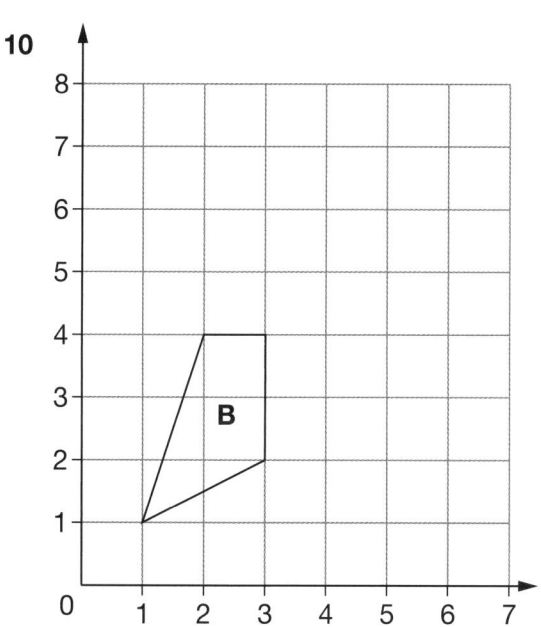

Draw the new position of shape B when it is translated (moved) right 3 and up 4.

11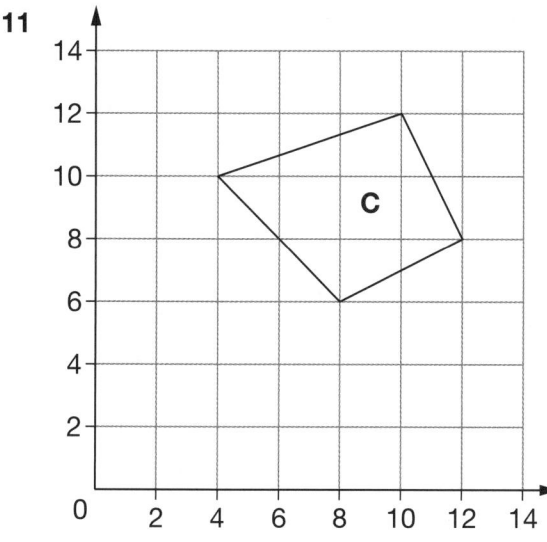

Draw the new position of shape C when it is translated (moved) left 2 and down 4.

In questions 12–15 each shape (**A**, **B**, **C** and **D**) has been moved to a new position (**A´**, **B´**, **C´** and **D´** respectively). Describe how each shape has been translated.

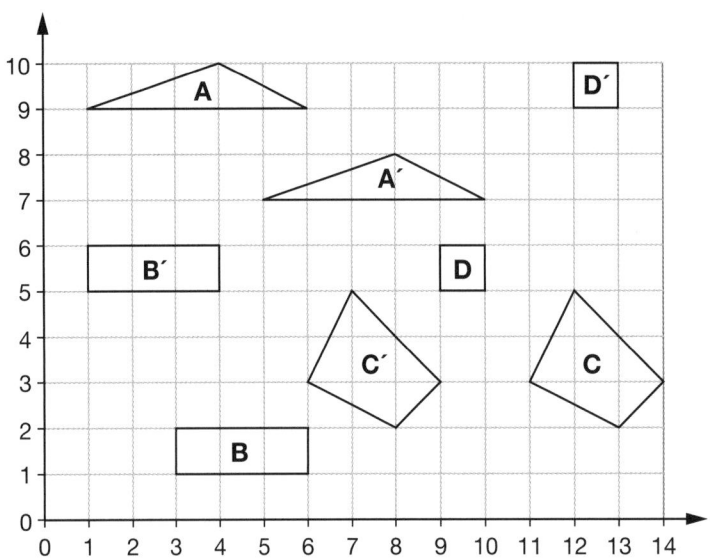

12 From **A** to **A´** ....

13 From **B** to **B´** ....

14 From **C** to **C´** ....

15 From **D** to **D´** ....

NVR Symmetry

Which pattern on the right is a reflection of the pattern on the left? Underline the answer.

16

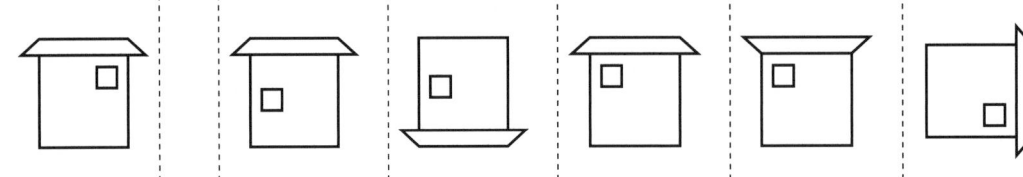

a   b   c   d   e

17

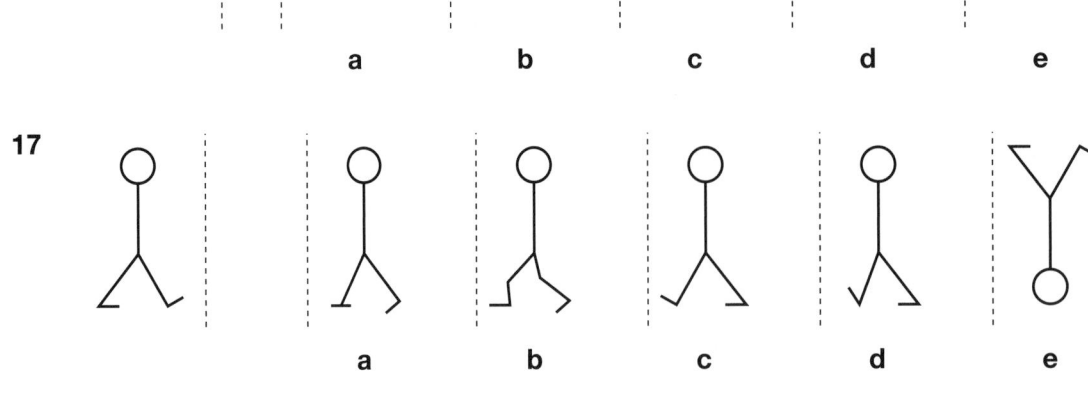

a   b   c   d   e

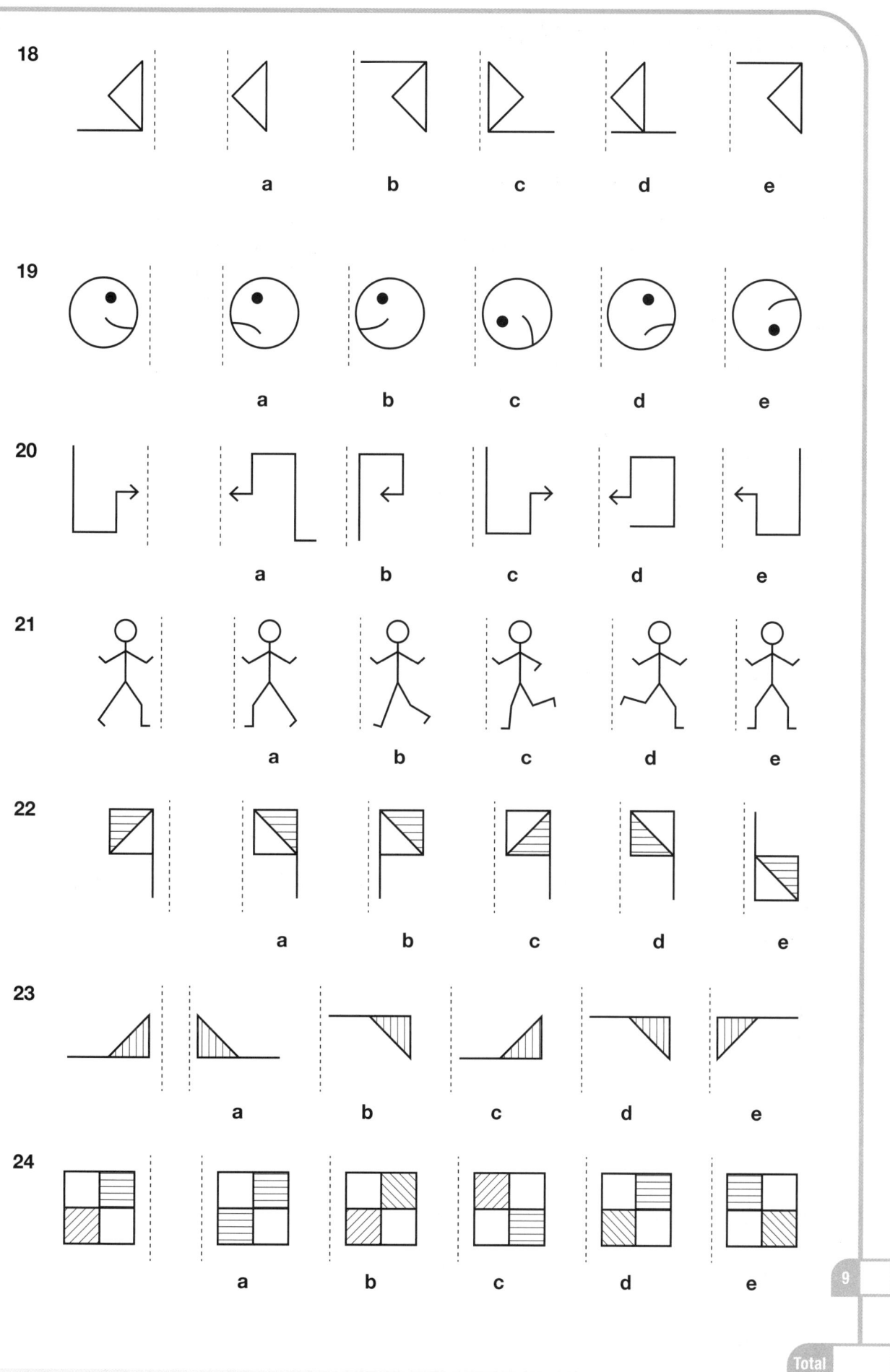

Measurement and Pairs

KEY SKILL

Check you know these units of measurement:

Length 1 km = 1000 m   1 m = 1000 mm
1 m = 100 cm   1 cm = 10 mm

Mass 1 kg = 1000 g   1 g = 1000 mg

Capacity 1 litre = 1000 ml

TOP TIP!
When working with metric measurements always check the number of zeros and the position of the decimal point carefully

Area is calculated by multiplying two lengths and it is given in square units, e.g. square cm (cm²), square metres (m²).

Volume is calculated by multiplying three lengths and it is given in cubic units, e.g. cubic cm (cm³), cubic metres (m³).

Time 1 week = 7 days   1 day = 24 hours
1 hour = 60 minutes   1 minute = 60 seconds

WORKED EXAMPLES

Which shape completes the second pair in the same way as the first pair?
Underline the answer.

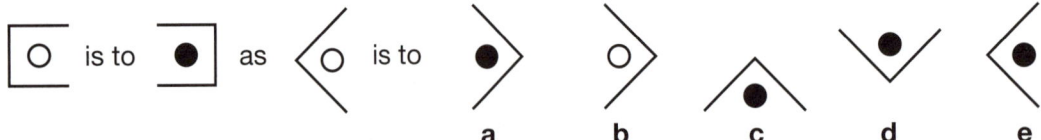

The second shape of the first pair has the line pattern reflected and the circle shading changed from white to black, so to complete the second pair the line pattern needs to be reflected and the white circle must be black. That is option a.

How many seconds are there in 1 hour and 1 minute?

1 hour is **60 minutes**, so there are 61 minutes; each minute has **60 seconds**;
so 61 × 60 = **3660 seconds**

⏱ 35 mins

Conversions

1   A candle burns at $\frac{1}{2}$ cm per hour. The candle is 20 cm tall when it is lit at 2 p.m.

   a   How tall will the candle be at 6 p.m.? ....

b How long will it take to burn 5 cm of the candle? ....

   c What time will it be when the candle is 16 cm tall? ....

2 Write these measurements in order, from biggest to smallest.

   250 ml   0.55 litres   1.2 litres   1250 ml   500 ml

   .... > .... > .... > .... > ....

3 Convert these measurements to metres.

   a 2 km ....   **b** 5000 mm ....

   c 350 cm ....   **d** 0.04 km ....

4 A chutney recipe uses three times as much apple as onion. Natalie uses 6 kg of apples to make some chutney. The recipe says to add 100 ml of vinegar for each kg of apples. One-and-a-half kilograms of apples will produce two jars of chutney.

   a What weight of onions are needed? ....

   b How much vinegar must be added? ....

   c How many jars of chutney will this mixture make? ....

Area and Perimeter

5 This diagram shows a garden. The path around the edge is 1 m wide.

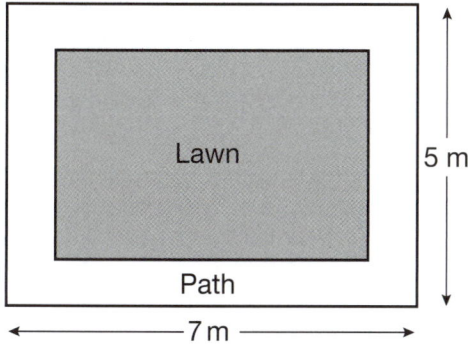

   What is the **area** of the lawn? ....

6 What is the **perimeter** of a rectangle 7 cm wide and 16 cm long? 1

7 What is the perimeter of a square with sides of 4.5 cm? 1

8 A window measures 100 cm × 120 cm.

    a What is the perimeter of the window? ....

    Its shutters are 5 cm larger than the window on each side,
as well as at the top and bottom.

    b What is the perimeter of the area covered by the shutters? 2

Volume

9 How many 250 ml bottles can be filled from
a catering container of squash containing $4\frac{1}{2}$ litres? 1

10 What is the **volume** of a shallow box which
measures 50 cm × 40 cm and which is 20 cm high? 1

11 A large cube is built out of small 1 cm cubes.
If the large cube has edges 10 cm long, how many
of the small 1 cm cubes will be needed to build it? 1

Time

12 A programme starts at 10.45 a.m. and ends
at 11.20 a.m. How long does the programme last? 1

13 If a bus leaves the station every 22 minutes, complete the departure times for
the next two buses:

    10:00, 10:22, 10:44, ..., ... 1

14 How many minutes are there in $1\frac{1}{4}$ hours? 1

15 Write $73\frac{1}{2}$ minutes as hours, minutes and seconds.

    .... hours .... minutes .... seconds 1

38

16 This table shows the weekly opening times of a shop.

Sunday	Closed
Monday	9.00 a.m. – 5.00 p.m.
Tuesday	10.00 a.m. – 6.00 p.m.
Wednesday	9.00 a.m. – 1.00 p.m.
Thursday	8.00 a.m. – 5.00 p.m.
Friday	8.30 a.m. – 4.30 p.m.
Saturday	9.00 a.m. – 12.00 noon

a What is the earliest time the shop opens?

....

b Which day does the shop stay open latest in the evening?

....

c Which day of the week is the shop open for the most hours?

....

d During one whole week, how many hours is the shop open for in total?

....

NVR Complete the Pair

Which shape completes the second pair in the same way as the first pair?
Underline the answer.

17

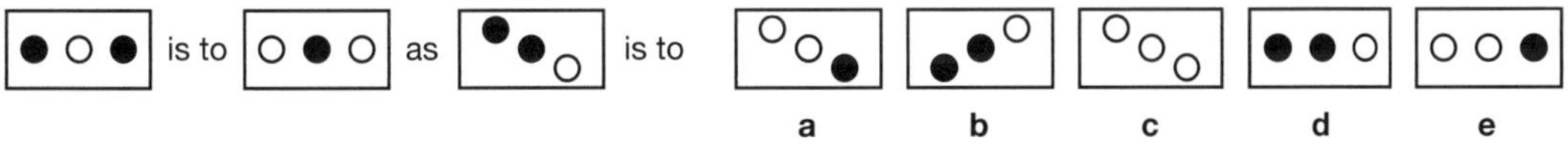

18

19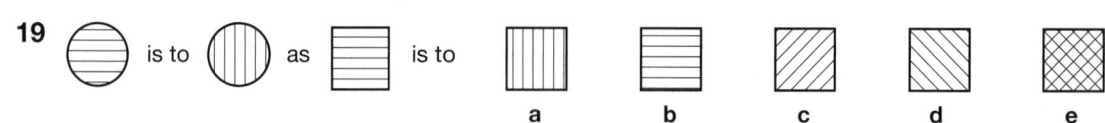

20

21

22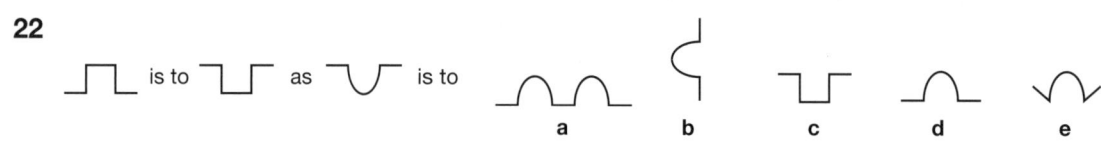

23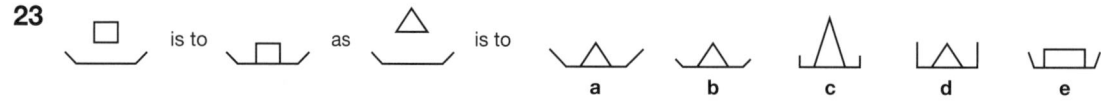

24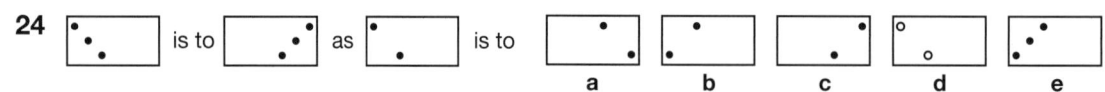

25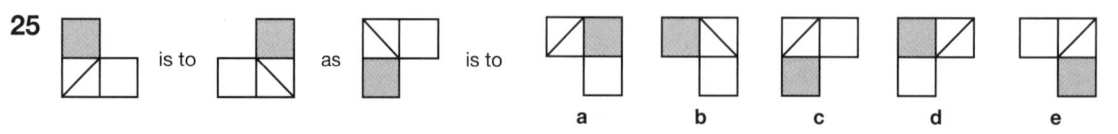

Statistics and Pattern Recognition

KEY SKILL

Statistics is all about working with sets of data. The data may take many forms and can be presented in many different ways. These include bar graphs, line graphs and tally charts. For each of these the axes of the graphs must be clearly labelled. So when taking information from a graph check the axes and any key carefully.

Another form of graph is a pictogram. A pictogram uses a picture or symbol to represent a certain number on a graph. Pictograms can sometimes use half of a symbol to represent half of the amount.

Tables and Venn diagrams are another way to record data. Check the headings and labels carefully when reading data from them, and if constructing them remember to label them clearly.

TOP TIP!

It can help to use a ruler when reading values off a graph

WORKED EXAMPLE

Which is the odd one out? Underline the answer.

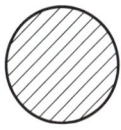  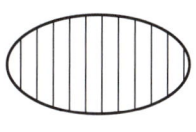 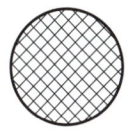 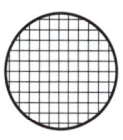

  a   b   c   d   e

This straightforward example shows that option c is an oval while the other shapes are all circles. So c is the odd one out. Notice that they all have different shading patterns, so that feature is not significant in identifying the odd one out.

Bar Charts

1 This graph records how many children selected each fruit as one of their favourites.

   a Which fruit was most popular?

   ....

   b Which was the least popular?

   ....

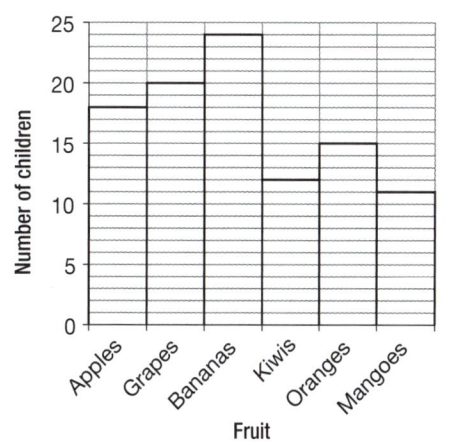

c How many children chose grapes? ....

d How many more children chose apples than oranges? ....

2 Toli recorded the amount of rain that fell during four weeks of his school holiday.

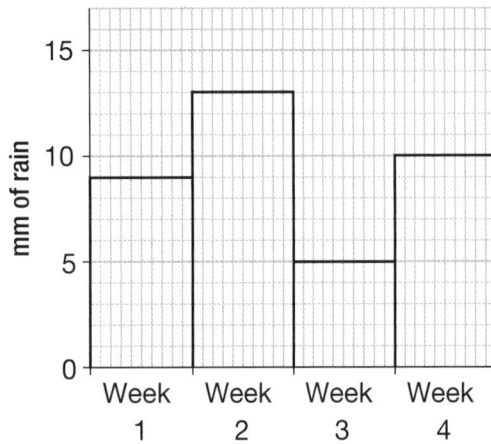

a How much rain fell in the first week?

....

b Which was the driest week?

....

c What was the total rainfall for the four weeks?

....

3 Use the information in this tally chart to plot the bar chart.

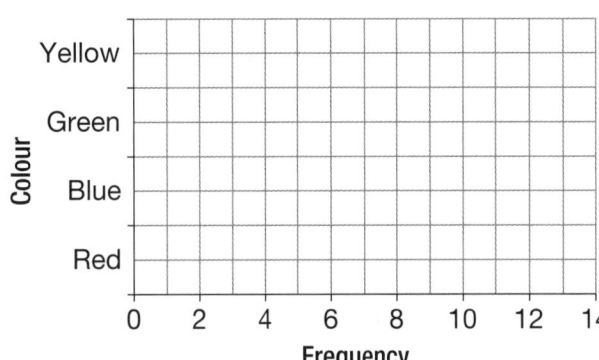

Red											
Blue								
Green							
Yellow									

Line Graphs

4
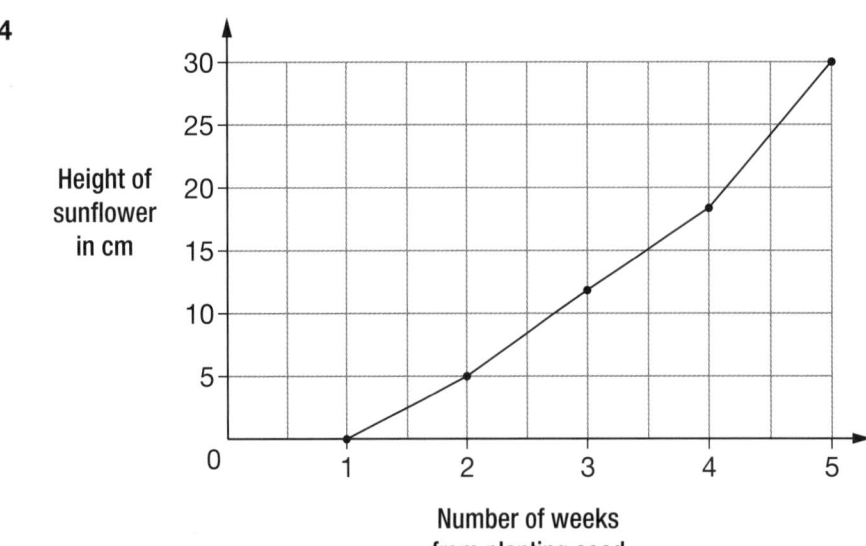

42

a How tall was the sunflower two weeks after it was planted? ....

b From the time it was planted, how many weeks did it take for the sunflower to grow to 30 cm? ....

Venn Diagrams

5 Look carefully at the overlapping groups in the diagram to work out the answers to the questions that follow.

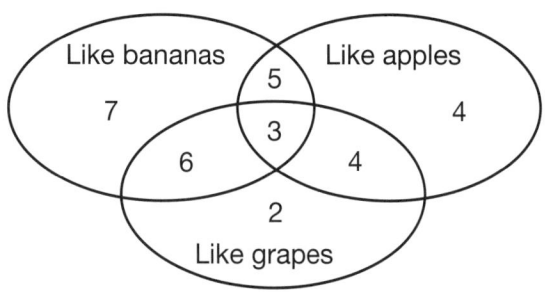

a How many children like apples and bananas but not grapes? ....

b How many children like grapes but not apples or bananas? ....

c How many children only like bananas? ....

d How many children like all three fruits? ....

e How many children like apples and grapes but not bananas? ....

f How many like grapes and bananas but not apples? ....

Pictograms

6

Team E: ○○○
Team D: ○○○○○○
Team C: ○○○○◐
Team B: ○○○○○
Team A: ○○○○○○◐

○ = 2 goals

The pictogram shows the number of goals that five different teams scored during a football competition.

a How many goals were scored by team D? ....

b How many more goals did team A score than team E? ....

c What was the difference between the number of goals scored by team B and team C? ....

Carroll Diagrams/Tables

7 This table shows the months in which children in a class have their birthday.

January	3	July	1
February	5	August	1
March	1	September	3
April	2	October	2
May	5	November	3
June	2	December	2

a If the data is for a whole class, how many children are there in the class?

....

b How many more birthdays are there in May than August? ....

c Which months have the most birthdays? ....

8 A bag of tile shapes was sorted. The red ones were separated from the other colours, and the square shapes were separated from the other shapes. The numbers were recorded below. Complete the table and then answer the questions.

	Square	Not square	Total
Red	14	32	
Not red	26	28	
Total			

a How many shapes were not squares? ....

b How many tiles were red? ....

c How many tiles were sorted all together? ....

NVR Odd One Out

Which is the odd one out? Underline the answer.

9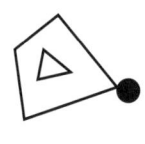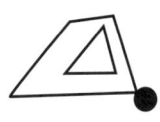
    a   b   c   d   e

10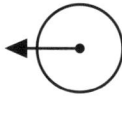
    a   b   c   d   e

11
    a   b   c   d   e

12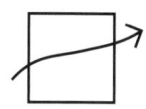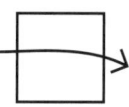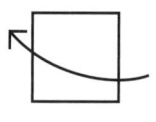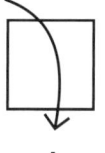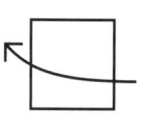
    a   b   c   d   e

13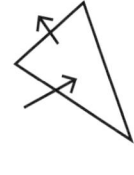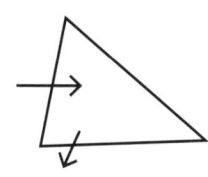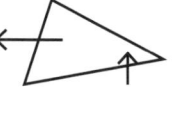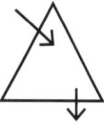
    a   b   c   d   e

14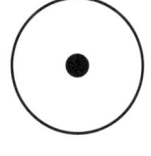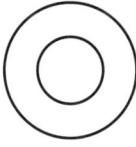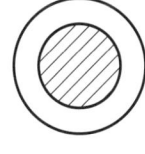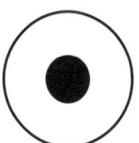
    a   b   c   d   e

15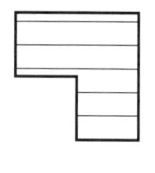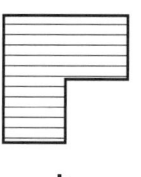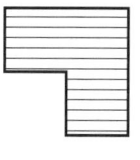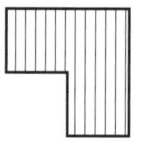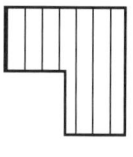
    a   b   c   d   e

Total 32

Curveball Questions 1

KEY SKILL

- Read the question carefully!
- What are you asked to do or to work out? What information have you been given?
- Work carefully and systematically.
- Check your answer at the end.

25 mins

1 Plot these points on the grid below:

A (2,4)   B (4,1)   C (8,2)   D (10,5)

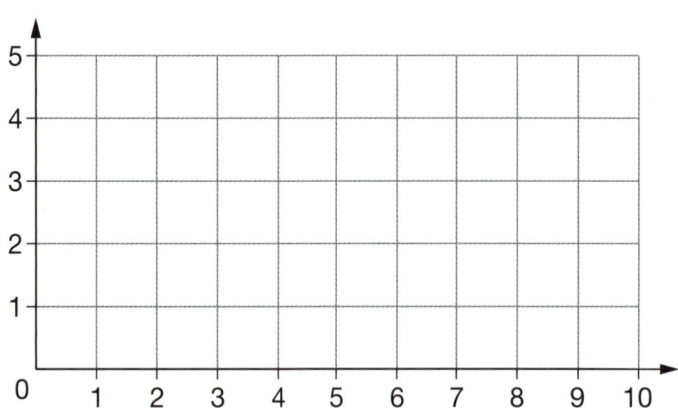

Plot point X at (2,3) and Y at (9,3). Join the two points X and Y with a straight line.

Give the coordinates of any point above the line XY and within the shape formed by ABCD.

....

5

2 This diagram shows which children had which pets. Transfer the information to the Venn diagram below by writing each name in the correct place.

	Has a cat	**Does not have a cat**
Has a dog	Tom, Ann, Mysha, Ed, Sam	Sue, Ted, Lee, Rob
Does not have a dog	Tess, Rino, Meg	Caz, Dot

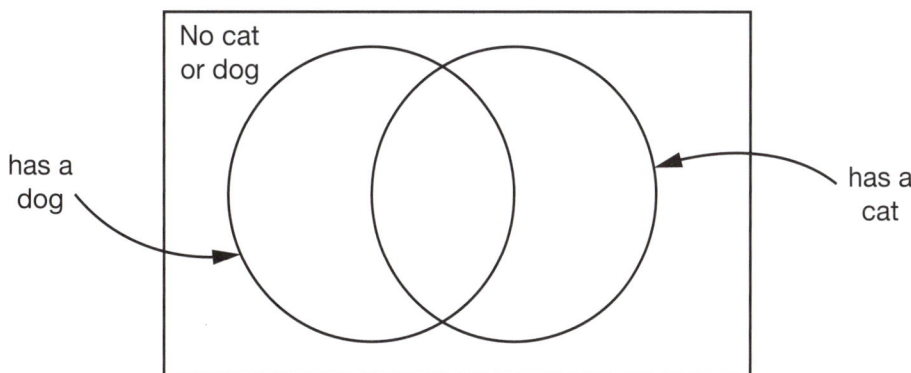

3 Complete the pattern below by reflecting it in the vertical and horizontal lines across the square.

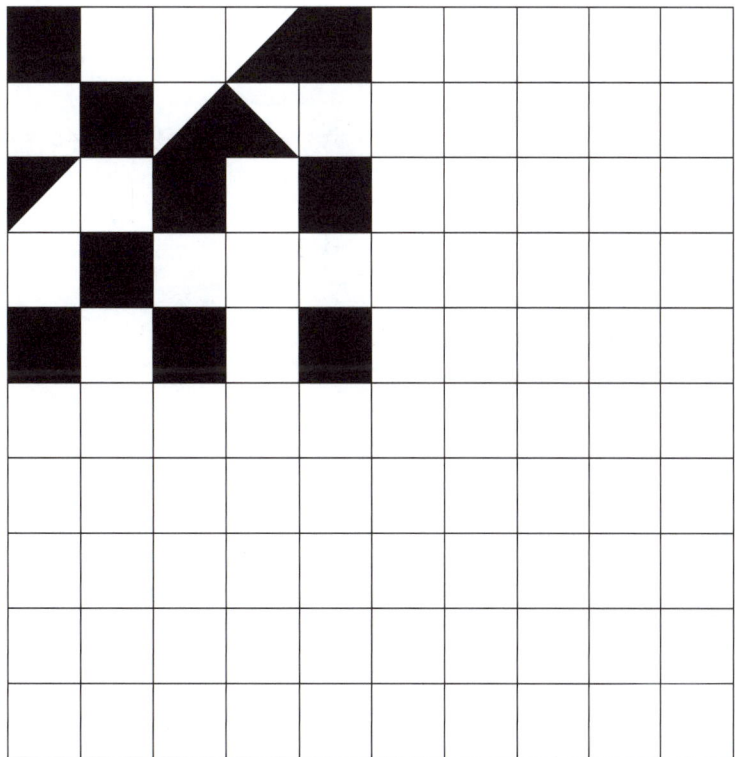

Mixed Papers

Mixed Paper 1

Number

1. Write in digits the number that has six tens, four thousands, nine units and two hundreds.

   ....

2. Add together the **digits** in the hundreds columns of these numbers:

   7856   461   5307   ....

3. Fill the gaps along this number chain:

   4 × 3 = ...÷ 2 = ...+ 32 = ...

4. Fill in the gaps.

   a 401 + ... = 722   b .... − 545 = 455

   c 72 ÷ .... = 12   d 352 × .... = 35200

5. What is the **difference** between 752 and 649? ....

6. $\frac{1}{2}$ of 4520 = ...

7. What is the **total** of $\frac{1}{4} + \frac{1}{2} + \frac{1}{8}$ = ...

8. If there are two halves in one whole, how many halves are there in $17\frac{1}{2}$.................

9. Underline the fractions below which are equivalent fractions.

   $\frac{6}{9}$ $\frac{1}{2}$ $\frac{2}{3}$ $\frac{4}{12}$ $\frac{5}{12}$ $\frac{20}{30}$

10 304.6 + ... = 320

11 Which number comes next? 6.4, 6.8, 7.2, 7.6, ...

12 What is the total of 3 × 9 and 7 × 20? ....

13 4250 × 5 = ...

14 20 103 × .... = 60 309

15 a 409.3 + 37 + 1285.6 = ...

b 4805 − 148 = ...

NVR Codes

Which code matches the shape or pattern given at the end of each line?
Underline the answer.

16

	CX	AZ	CY	BX	BY
	a	b	c	d	e

AX   AY   BY   CZ   ?

17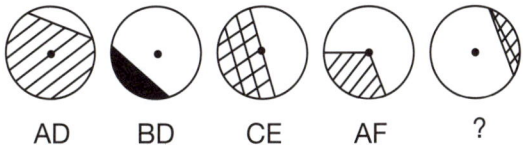

	BF	AE	CD	BE	CF
	a	b	c	d	e

AD   BD   CE   AF   ?

18

	GY	EZ	DZ	EY	DY
	a	b	c	d	e

DX   EZ   FY   EX   GZ   ?

19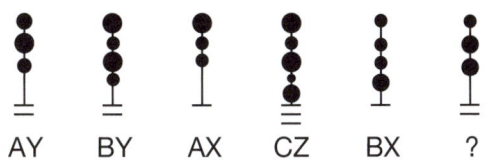

	BZ	CX	AZ	CY	AY
	a	b	c	d	e

AY   BY   AX   CZ   BX   ?

Word and Logic Problems

20 A bookcase has five shelves and each shelf is 2 m long. On average, 6 books take up 20 cm of space along a shelf. If the shelves are full, how many books can fit into the whole bookcase?

....

21 There are six shops in the High Street. The butcher is next to the newsagent and the toy shop. The hairdresser is next to the toy shop and at the end of the street. The greengrocer is next to the fish and chip shop and four doors away from the hairdresser. Which shop is on the other side of the greengrocer?

....

22 A cake stall has 24 scones, 24 iced buns and 24 eclairs at the beginning of the day. All of the scones, half of the iced buns and a quarter of the eclairs have been sold by 11 a.m. How many items have been sold altogether?

....

NVR Grids

Which pattern completes the larger shape or grid? Underline the answer.

23

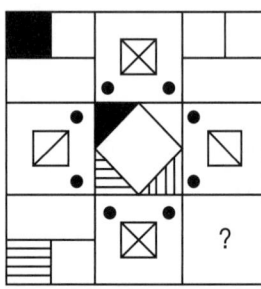   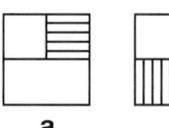 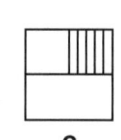 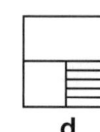 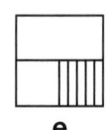
         a   b   c   d   e

24

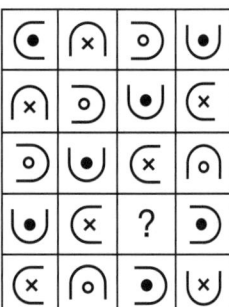
         a   b   c   d   e

25

26

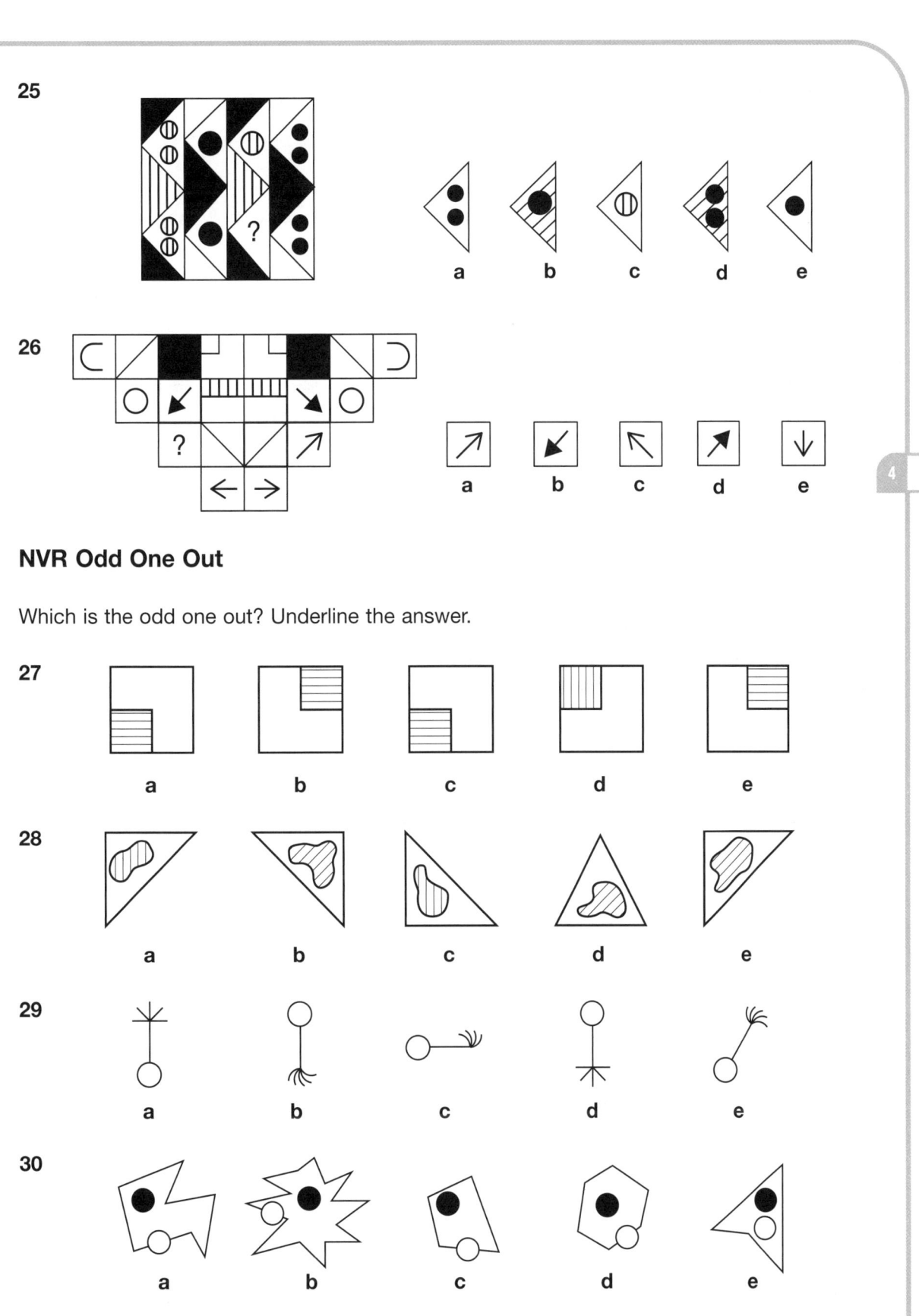

NVR Odd One Out

Which is the odd one out? Underline the answer.

27

28

29

30

31

Area and Perimeter

32 What is the **perimeter** of a rectangle 13 cm long and 5 cm wide? ....

33 A rectangular allotment has a perimeter of 450 m. If it is 50 m wide, how long is it?

....

34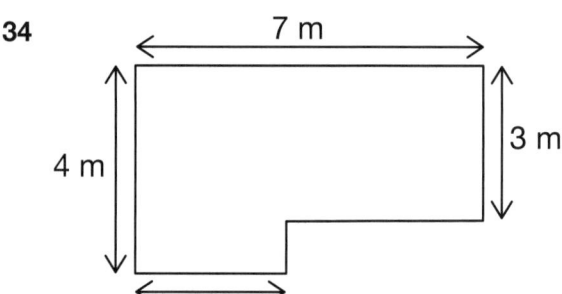

This is a plan of Jane's kitchen. What is the **area** of the floor?

....

35 How many square metre stone slabs are needed for a patio 4 m × 5 m and the path leading to the patio which is 1 m wide and 6 m long? ....

Statistics

36 The number of children's meals sold at a burger bar is recorded over four days.

Each 😊 represents four children's meals.

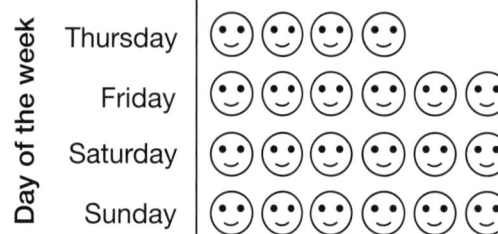

a How many children's meals were sold on Friday? ....

b How many more were sold on Sunday than Thursday? ....

c How many children's meals were sold altogether over the four days? ....

Total 42

Mixed Paper 2

Number

1 409 – 173 = ...

2 67 + 22 = 100 – ....

3 673 + 22 = 1000 – ....

Maths Sequences

Fill in the missing numbers in these sequences.

TOP TIP!
When numbers increase in a sequence, they have been added to or multiplied. When they decrease, they have been subtracted from or divided

4 740   650   560   380   ....

5 22   29   36   43   ....

6 43.7   44.6   45.5   ....   47.3   ....

7 1   2   6   120   720   5040

NVR Similarities

Which shape or pattern on the right belongs with the group on the left? Underline the answer.

8
                                                     a   b   c   d   e

9
                                                     a   b   c   d   e

10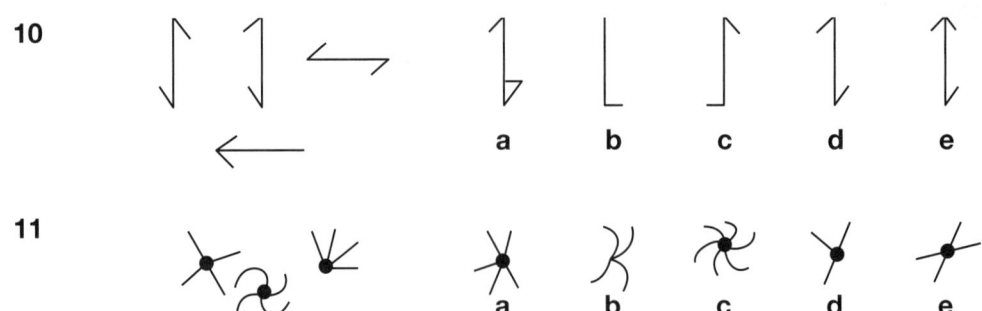

11

NVR Codes

Which code matches the shape or pattern given at the end of each line? Underline the answer.

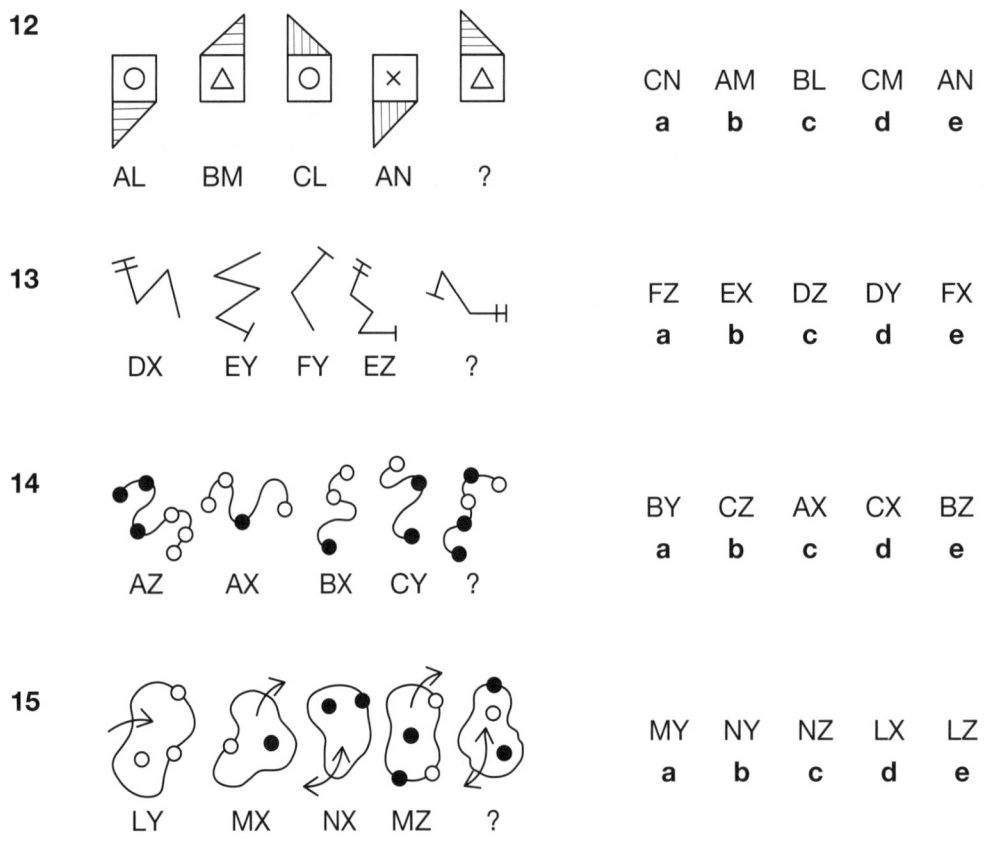

Shapes

16 Which of the following triangles are scalene triangles? Underline them.

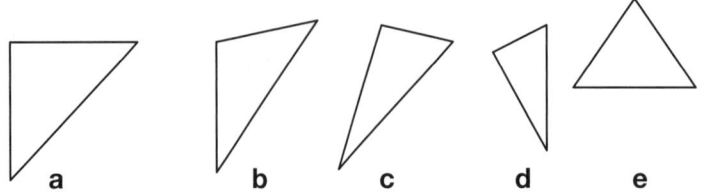

17 A cuboid has how many of the following?

  a Faces .... **b** Edges .... **c** Vertices ....

18 Name the shapes.

  a Has four equal-length sides and four right angles. ....

  b Has six sides. ....

  c A quadrilateral with parallel opposite sides and no right angles. ....

  d Has five equal-length sides. ....

19 Identify which of these shapes have lines of symmetry and draw one line of symmetry across them.

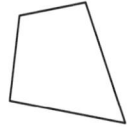 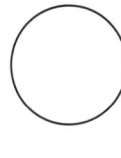  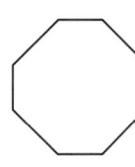 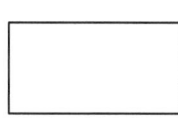 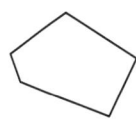

  a   b   c   d   e   f

Coordinates

20 a Give the coordinates of the following points on the graph below:

  A ....   **B** ....

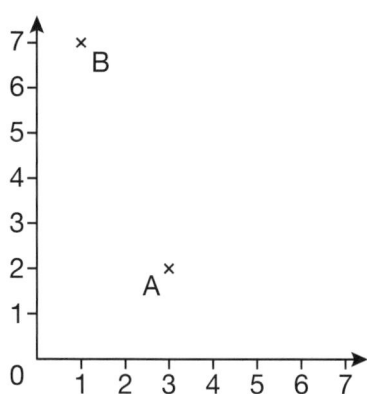

  b Plot these points on the same graph and join them together: X (2,4), Y (2,6), Z (5,6).

  c Name the type of shape that is formed ....

21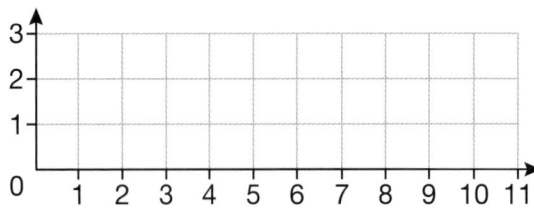

Plot the points (3,1) and (9,3) and join them together.

Give the coordinates of the point halfway along the line. ....

22 Plot the following points on the graph below and join them in that order.

(2,3) (2,5) (4,6) (6,6) (8.5) (8,3) (6,2) (4,2)

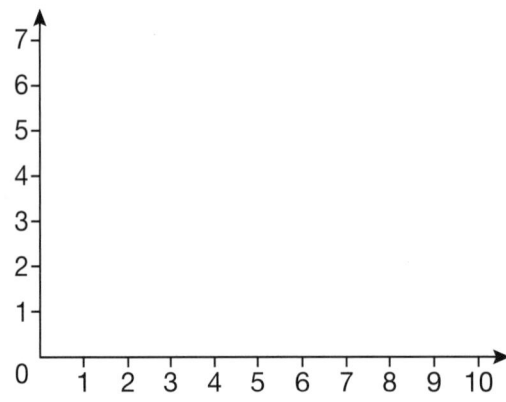

a Give the coordinates of the point at the centre of the shape. ....

b If a vertical line of symmetry is drawn through the shape, give the coordinates of two points on that line. ....

NVR Complete the Pair

Which shape or pattern on the right completes the second pair in the same way as the first pair? Underline the answer.

Example

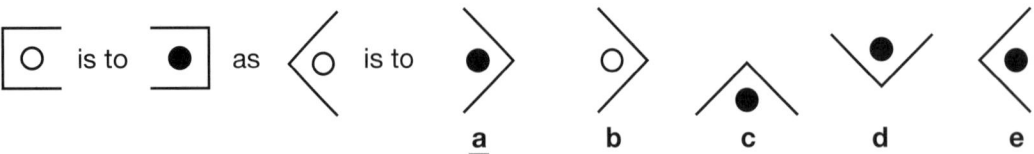

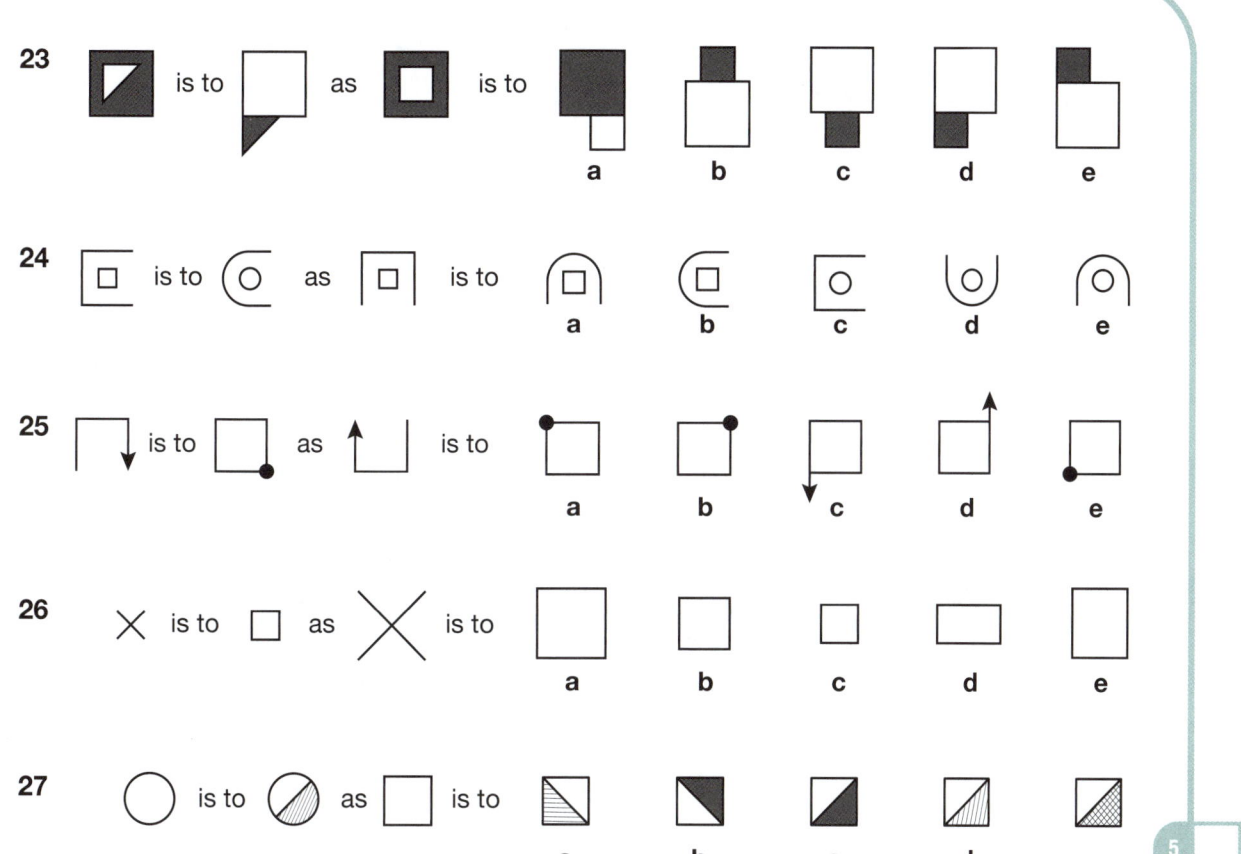

Venn Diagrams

28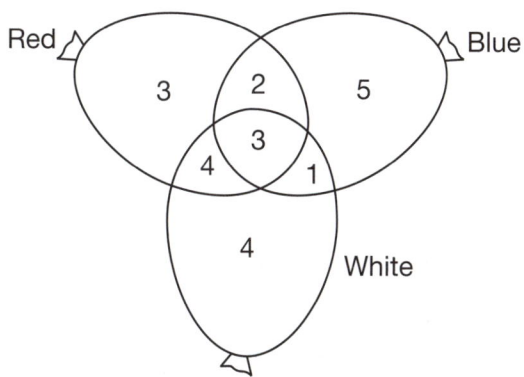

There are 22 packs of balloons. Some of the packs contain balloons that are all the same colour (either red or blue or white), some have just two of the three colours, and some have all three colours. From the diagram above answer these questions.

a How many packs have just white balloons? ....

b How many packs have just red and blue balloons? ....

c How many packs have all three colours in them? ....

d How many packs altogether have just one colour? ....

e How many packs have some or all blue balloons? ....

f How many packs have two different colours in them? ....

Fractions

29 What fraction of each shape below is shaded? Simplify your answer where possible.

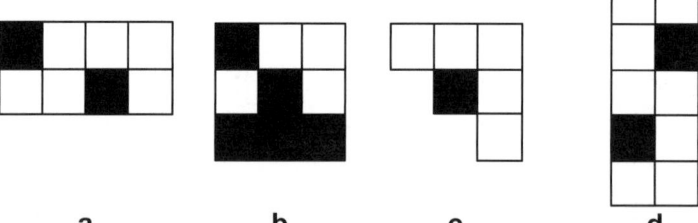

a   b   c   d

a ....   b ....   c ....   d ....

30 $45 - 7\frac{1}{2} =$ ....

31 $3\frac{1}{2} + 5\frac{1}{2} +$ .... $+ 4 = 17\frac{1}{2}$

Carroll Diagrams

32 This diagram records how many children in a class liked pasta and or pizza.

	Likes pasta	Doesn't like pasta
Likes pizza	14	10
Doesn't like pizza	8	4

a How many children are there in the class? ....

b Which is more popular, pasta or pizza? ....

c What fraction of the class do not like pizza? ....

Mixed Paper 3

Number

Fill in the missing numbers.

1 1456 = 1021 + 350 + ...

2 475 – .... = 360

3 6830.54   5829.76

    a What is the sum of the digits in the
hundreds columns of these two numbers? ....

    b What is the difference between the digits
in the tenths columns of these two numbers? ....

4 Write the following numbers in digits:

    a Seven million, four hundred and twenty thousand,
one hundred and thirty-three and five tenths. ....

    b Two thousand, seven hundredths, three
hundreds, six tenths and four units. ....

NVR Sequences

Which pattern or shape on the right continues or completes the sequence on the left?
Underline the answer.

5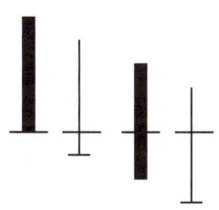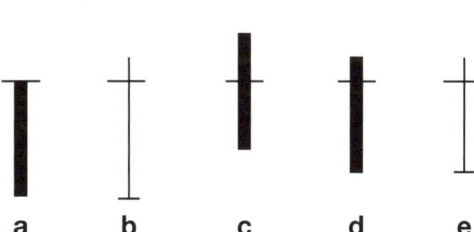

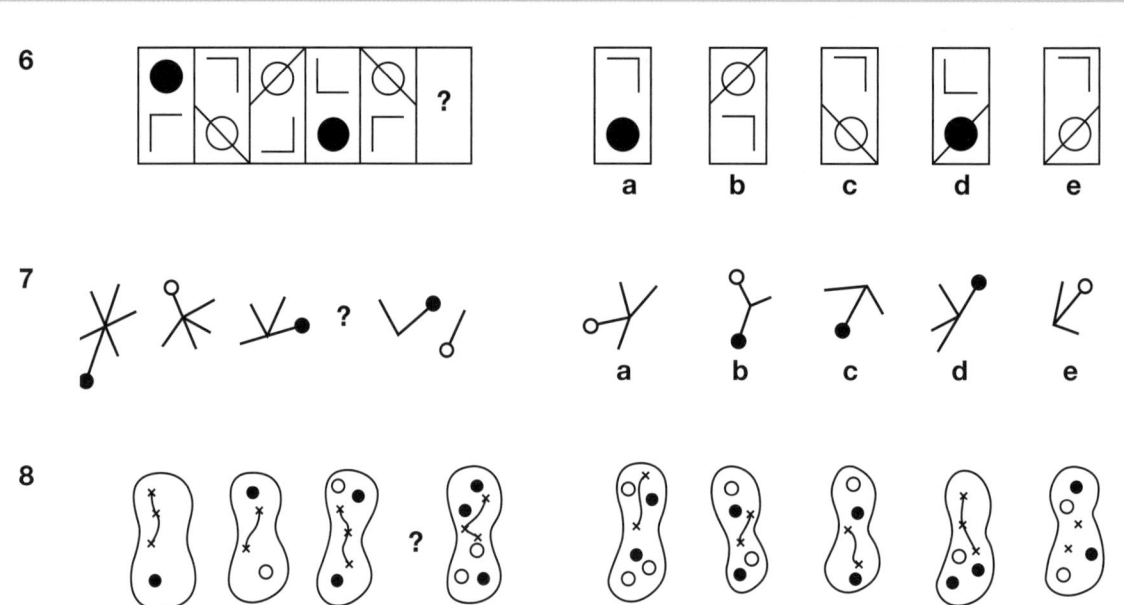

Symmetry

Which shape or pattern on the right is a reflection of the shape on the left? Underline the answer.

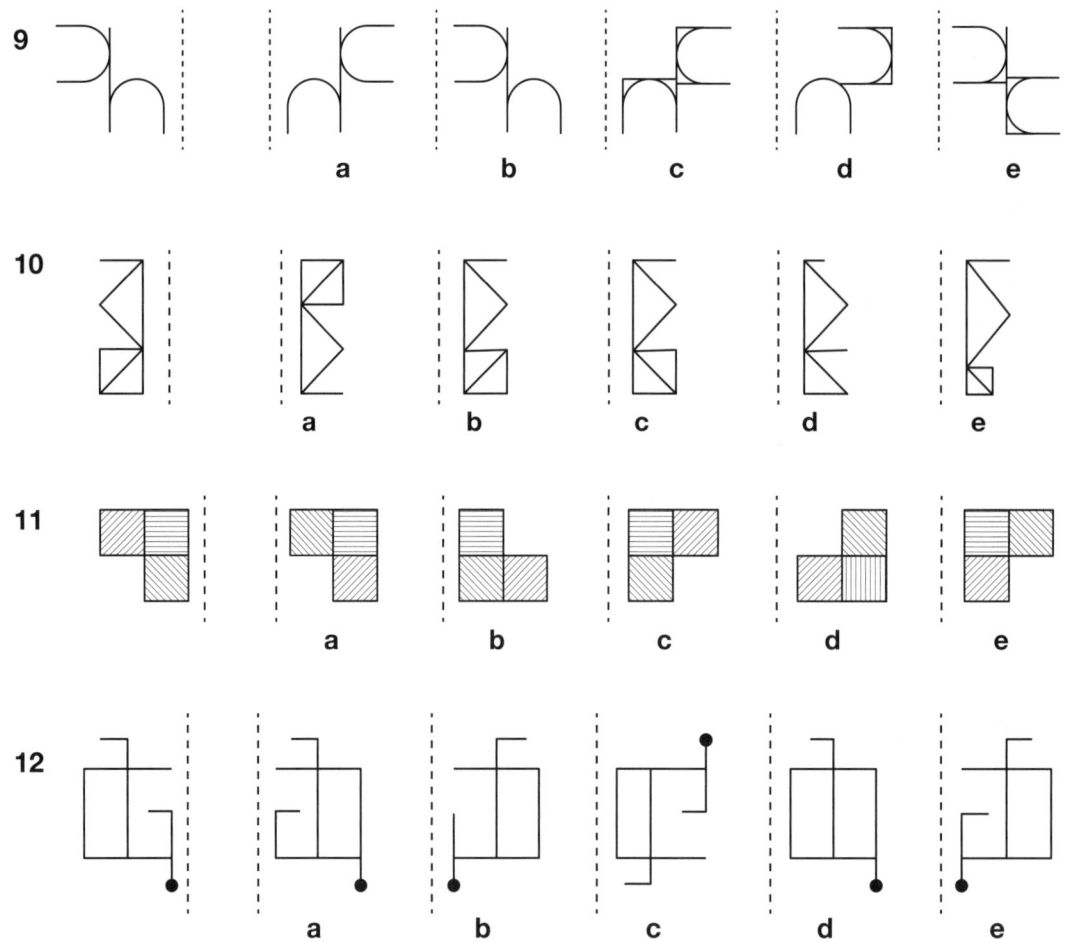

NVR Grids

Which shape or pattern on the right completes the grid on the left? Underline the answer.

13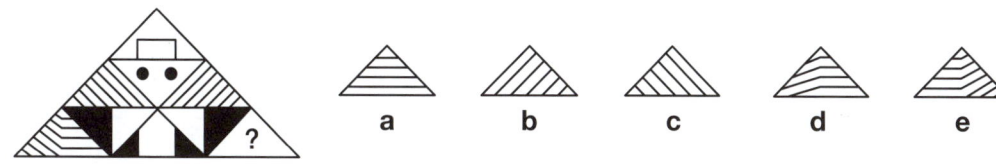

14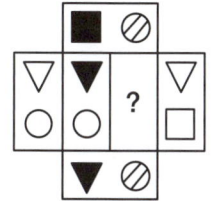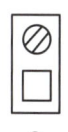

                                  a   b   c   d   e

Coordinates

15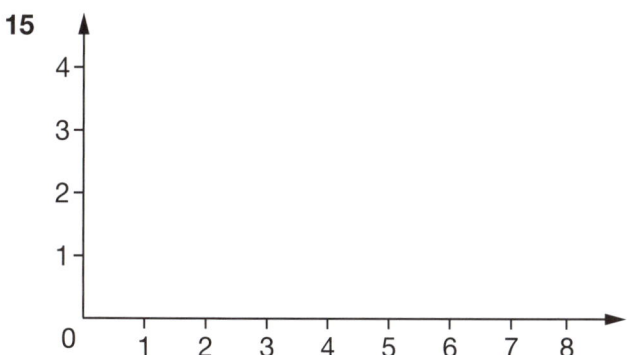

Name the shape that is formed when these **coordinates** are plotted on the grid above.

(1,1) (2,3) (6,1) (7,3) ....

16 What are the coordinates of points A, B, C and D?

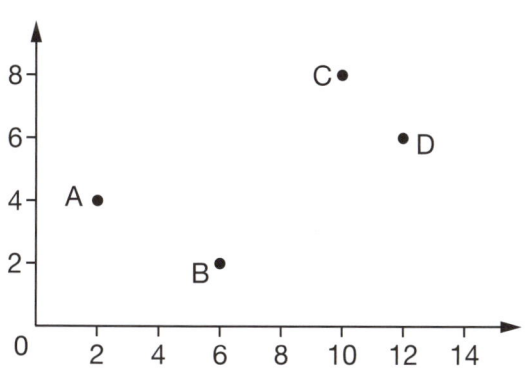

A .... B .... C .... D ....

17 On the grid below:

  a plot the points (1,2) and (9,4) and join them together with a straight line

  b plot the points (4,4) and (7,1) and join them together with a straight line

  c give the coordinates of the point where the two lines cross   ....

  d draw a horizontal line through the crossing point.
  Give the coordinates of any two points on that horizontal line   ....

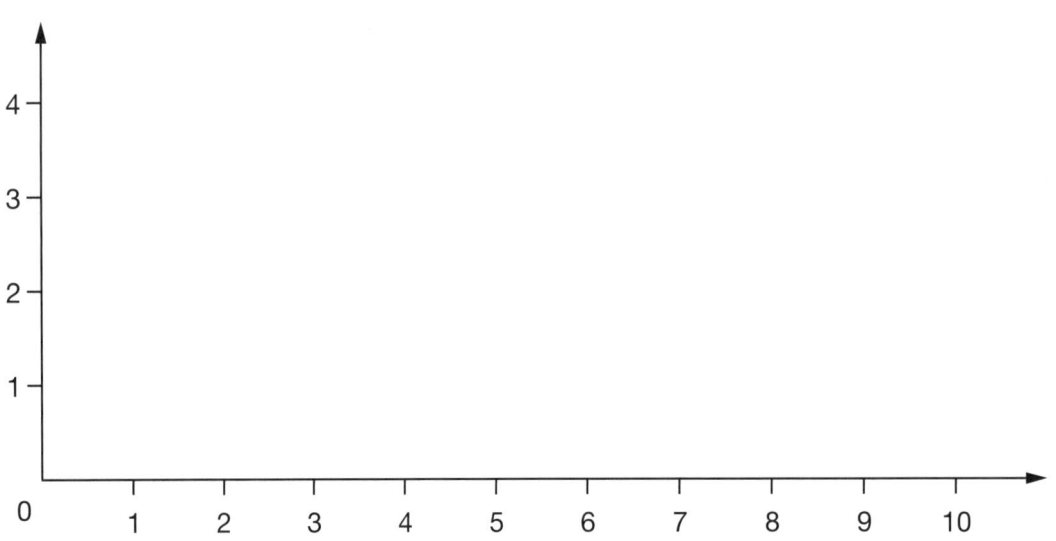

Measurement

18 500g of cake mixture makes 24 muffins. A bakery makes up 2kg of mixture.

How many muffins will the bakery make? ....

19 Tom has a tube of toothpaste which contains 200g of toothpaste. Each time he brushes his teeth he uses 5g of toothpaste. Tom brushes his teeth twice a day.

  a How many days will the tube last Tom?   ....

  b How much toothpaste does Tom use in 3 days?   ....

20 What is the **perimeter** of a regular pentagon with sides $17\frac{1}{2}$cm long? ....

21 A square field has a perimeter of 860 m.

 a What is the length of each side? ....

 b How many metres of wire will a farmer need to
 make a three-strand fence all round the field? ....

22 A pack of grass seed will cover 6 square
metres. How many packs are needed
to cover a lawn 8 m long and 3 m wide? ....

23 During the morning a train leaves the station every 12 minutes, with the first train leaving at 09:05. At what times will trains depart between 9 a.m. and 10 a.m.?

....

Line graphs

24 Ben starts walking from home at 9 a.m. The graph shows the distance he covers during his walk.

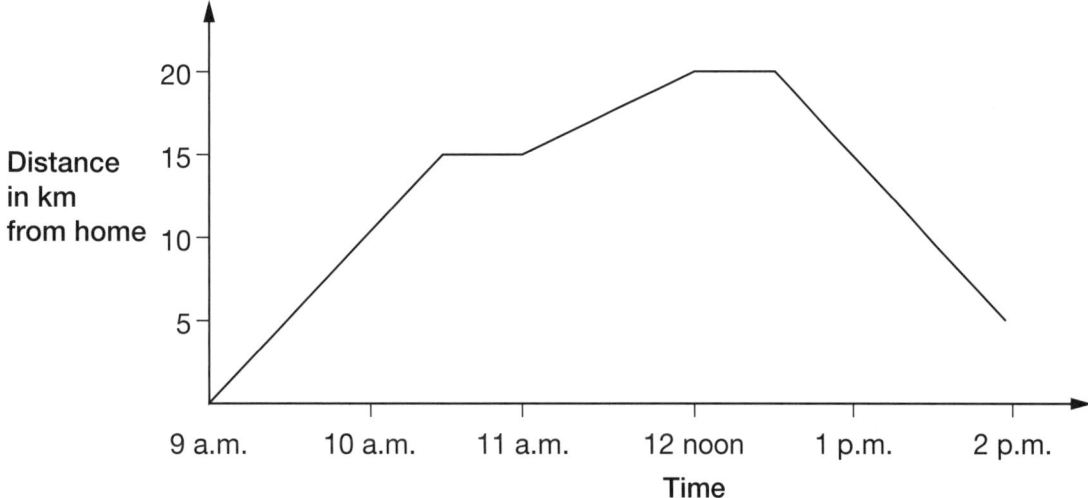

 a How far had he walked after one hour? ....

 b What time did he stop for his first rest? ....

 c How far from home was he at 1 p.m.? ....

Word and Logic Problems

25 Tanya saves £4.25 every week towards a new pair of shoes. After six weeks she has enough money to buy them. If she is left with £2.25, how much were the shoes?

   ....

26 A family are setting off on their holiday. They leave the house and get to the bus stop at 8.40 a.m. They wait to catch the bus to the station. They arrive at the station ten minutes before the 9.35 a.m. train leaves. If the bus journey was 32 minutes, how long did they wait for the bus?

   ....

27 Concert tickets cost £2.75 each. When buying tickets for a group, one ticket is given free for every ten tickets required.

   a How much is paid for the tickets for a group of 20? ....

   b How much has been saved? ....

Number

28 836 × 9 = ...

29 £6026 is shared equally between four people. How much do they each get?

   ....

30 .... × 3 = 360 ÷ 5

31 What number is five hundredths and three tens more than 52.58? ....

32 **a** When 3057 is divided by 100, what digit is in the tenths column? ....

   b When 8204 is multiplied by 100, what digit is in the thousands column? ....

Total 40

Mixed Paper 4

Number

1 Fill in the missing numbers.

   a 34 + ... = 4 less than (6 × 12)

   b 4922 − 768 = ...

   c $\frac{1}{2}$ of .... = 96 ÷ 4

NVR Sequences

Which shape or pattern on the right continues or completes the sequences on the left? Underline the answer.

2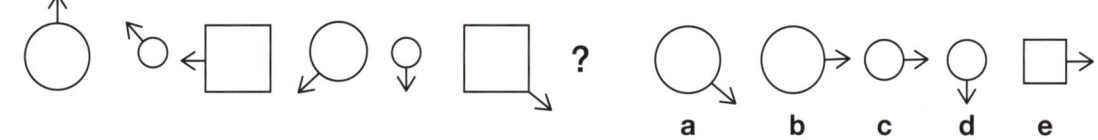

3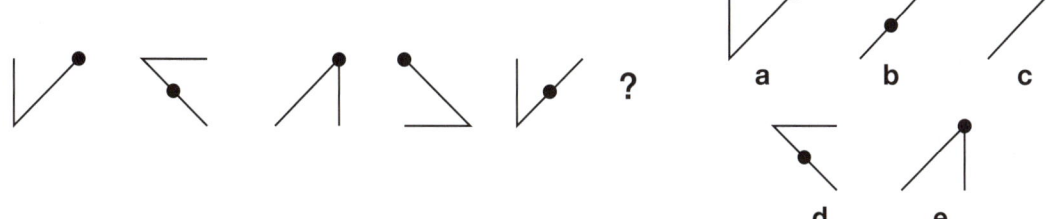

4

5

NVR Similarities

Which shape or pattern on the right belongs to the group on the left? Underline the answer.

6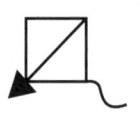
                                                  a   b   c   d   e

7
                                                  a   b   c   d   e

8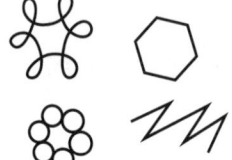
                                                a   b   c   d   e

9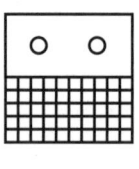
                                                a   b   c   d   e

Shape and Space

10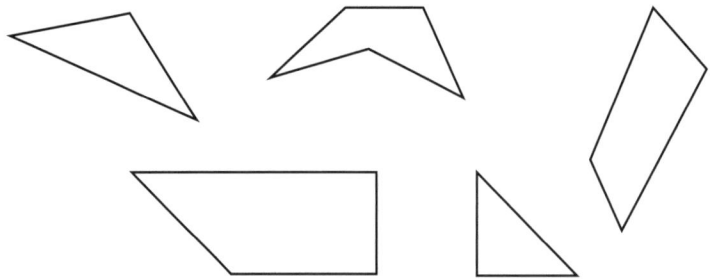

In the shapes drawn above:

    a put a tick in all of the angles that are acute angles

    b mark any right angles with a small square.

11 A runner goes round a rectangular track three times, and he ends up facing the same direction as when he started.

   a Through how many right angles has he turned?......................................

   b How many degrees is that in total? ....

12 Draw a quadrilateral which has one or more obtuse angles, marking the obtuse angle or angles with an X.

13 How many degrees does the minute hand of a clock move through between five o'clock and half past five? ....

Position and Direction

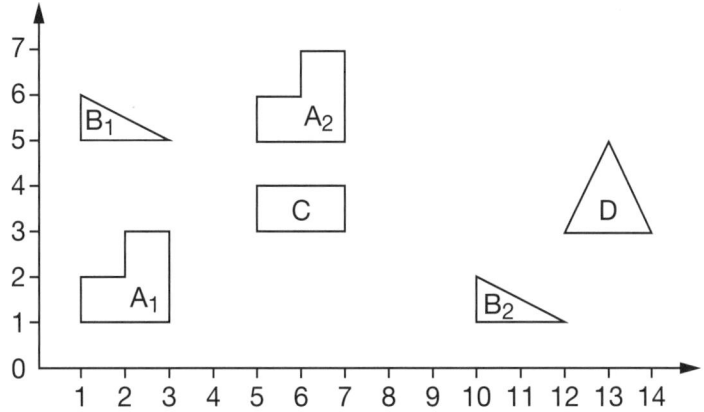

14 Describe the translation (movement) of shape A1 to A2. ....

15 Describe the translation of shape B1 to B2. ....

16 Translate shape C by right 6 and up 3. Draw the new position and label C2 ....

17 Translate shape D by left 5 and down 2. Draw the new position and label D2 ....

Measurement

18 How tall is a box which has a volume of 640 cubic cm if it is 8 cm long and 8 cm wide?

....

19 How many 10 cm cubes will fit into a box measuring 70 cm × 50 cm × 80 cm?

....

20 A tank takes 500 litres of fuel. If a household uses 250 ml per day, how much is left in the tank after 4 weeks? ....

21 1000 litres of water occupies 1 cubic metre. An underground water storage tank is 34 cubic metres. How many millions of ml will it hold when it is completely full?

....

Statistics

22 This graph shows the number of songs five boys have on their smartphones.

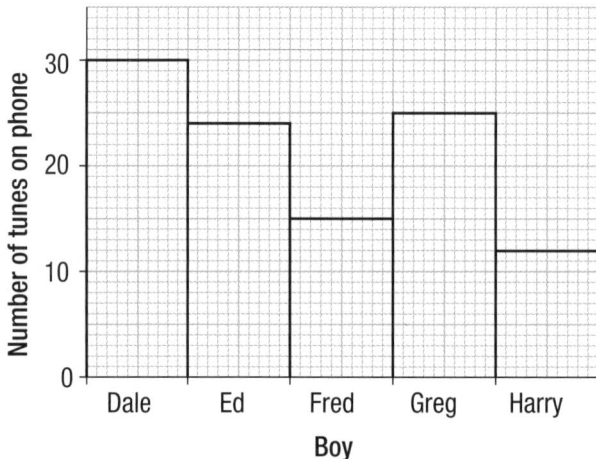

a How many songs do Harry and Fred have between them? ....

b How many more songs does Harry need in order to have 25 in total? ....

23 The diagram shows the data about the pets owned by 20 children.

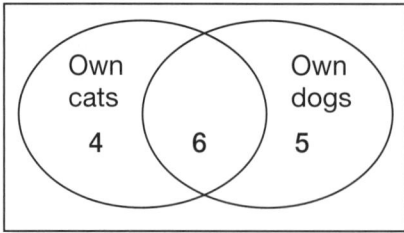

a How many children have cats and dogs? ....

b What fraction of the class only have dogs? Simplify your answer. ....

Number Skills

24 Which of the following fractions are equivalent to $\frac{1}{4}$? Underline them.

$\frac{4}{14}$ $\frac{5}{20}$ $\frac{6}{18}$ $\frac{7}{28}$ $\frac{4}{10}$ $\frac{3}{12}$

25 What is the total of $\frac{1}{2}$ of 52 and $\frac{1}{3}$ of 63? ....

26 Agatha has £500. She gives $\frac{1}{2}$ of it to charity A, $\frac{1}{4}$ of it to charity B and $\frac{1}{5}$ to charity C.

  a How much does each charity receive?

  A.......................   B.......................   C.......................

  b How much does she have left? ....

Measurements

27 Complete the following table.

A.m. or p.m. times	24-hour clock	Time written in words
		Three o'clock in the morning
	10:15	
4.25 p.m.		
		Half past eleven at night

28 There are four lessons each morning at school with a 20-minute break halfway through the morning. Lessons start at 09:00 and each lesson is 45 minutes long.

  a What time does the break start? ....

  b What is the time at the end of the four morning lessons? ....

29 How many seconds are there in 40 minutes?   ....

30 A ferry is scheduled to leave at 13:00 hours on Friday. The crossing should take six hours. A storm delays departure by 45 minutes and sailing takes 30 minutes longer than usual. When will it arrive at its destination?   ....

Total 40

Finished these Mixed Papers? Go online at www.bond11plus.co.uk and register for FREE RESOURCES to get two additional Mixed Papers.

Curveball Questions 2

1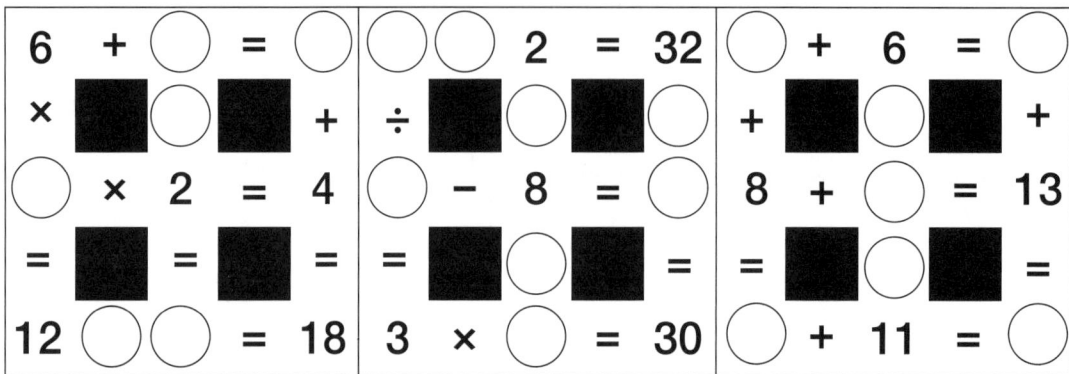

Complete the gaps in the number puzzles by filling in the missing numbers and signs.

2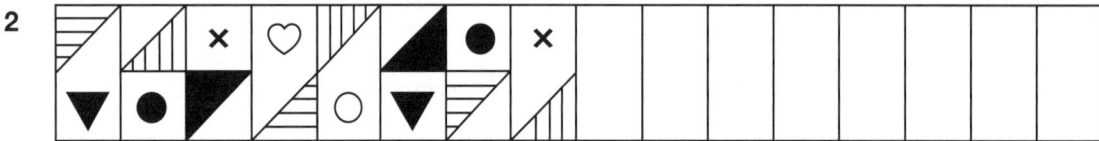

Continue the repeating pattern to complete the long rectangle.

3 A group of friends are leaving from the same place and planning to meet up for a picnic. One group is walking to the picnic site, one group is cycling and one group is going by car. The picnic site is 10 km away. The walkers average 5 km per hour, the cyclists travel at 25 km per hour and the car drives at 40 km per hour.

a When must they all leave in order to arrive together at 1 p.m.?

Walkers .... Cyclists .... Driving by car ....

b If they all set off at 3 p.m. for the return trip, when will the cyclists get back?

....

Total 20

Test Papers

Test Paper 1

1 Add together the digits in the hundreds and hundredths columns of these numbers:

   a 4860.37 ....

   b 520.041 ....

2 What is the difference between the digits in the tenths column and the tens column in these numbers?

   a 7450.25 ....

   b 7321.93 ....

3 Write the number seven million, three hundred and one thousand, twenty-four and nine tenths in digits. ....

4 Complete the number chain.

   42 + 6 .... ÷ 8 .... − 4 .... + 134 ....

5 359 + ... = 500

6 What are the next two numbers these sequences?

   a 4   7   10   13   ....

   b 63   57   51   45   ....

7 Fill the gaps in this sequence.

   115   130   160   175   ....

8 What is a quarter of a half of 400? ....

9 Complete these fractions.

$$\frac{\Box}{8} = \frac{6}{12} = \frac{5}{\Box} = \frac{\Box}{14} = \frac{50}{\Box}$$

Which shape or pattern on the right belongs to the group on the left?
Underline the answer.

10

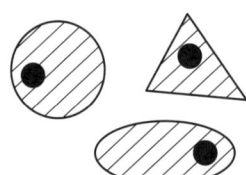

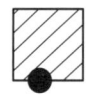    
   a   b   c   d   e

11

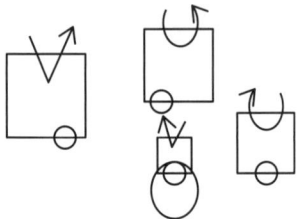

                          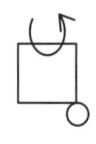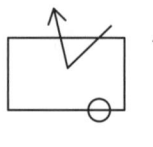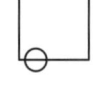
   a   b   c   d   e

12

  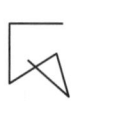 
   a   b   c   d   e

13

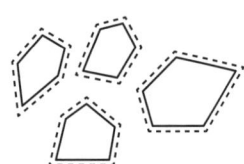

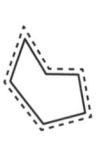 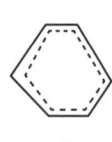 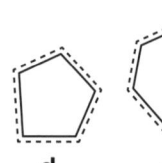
   a   b   c   d   e

Which shape or pattern on the right completes the grid on the left?
Underline the answer.

14

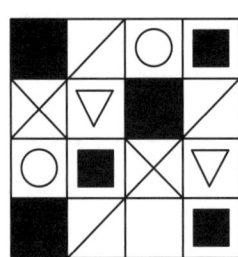

   a   b   c   d   e

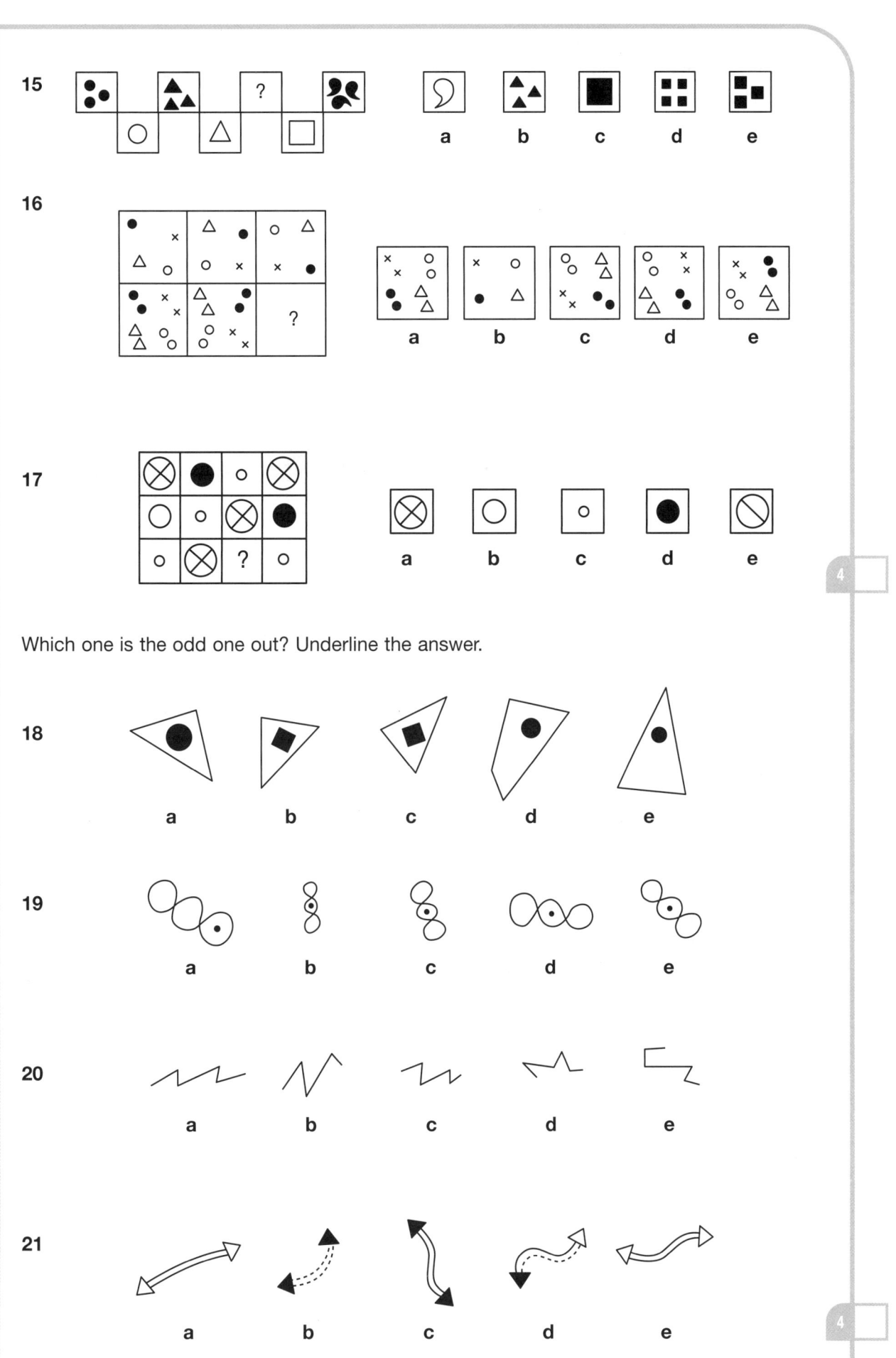

Which one is the odd one out? Underline the answer.

Which shape or pattern on the right completes the second pair in the same way as the first pair? Underline the answer.

22

23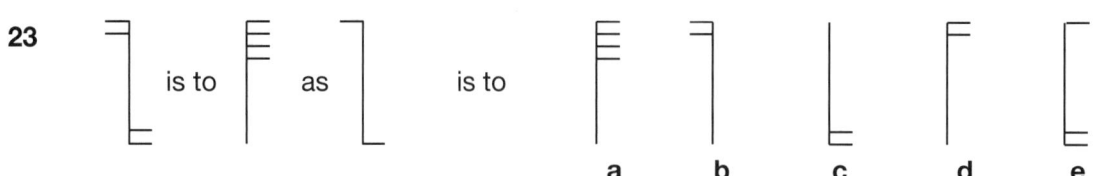

24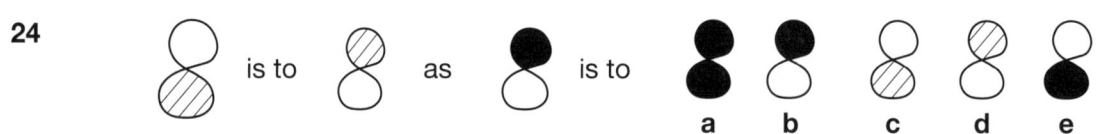

25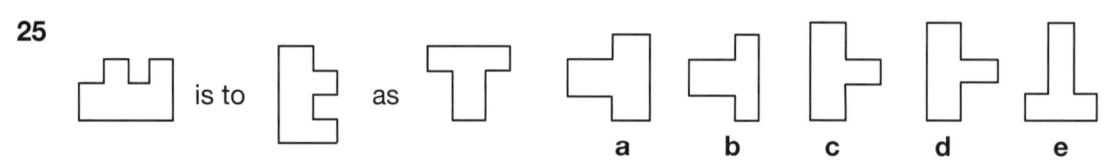

26 A television programme starts at 6.30 p.m. and ends at 7.20 p.m. During the programme there are two breaks for advertisements, each break is three minutes long. How long is the programme? ....

27 Carl compares the temperature in three different countries at the same time of day. Country A is 6 degrees cooler than country B and 8 degrees warmer that country C. If the temperature in country C is 7°C what is the temperature in country B? ....

28 A tin of mixed biscuits has 10 cream biscuits, 8 chocolate biscuits, 6 ginger biscuits and the rest are plain. One-quarter of the tin is chocolate biscuits.

   a How many biscuits are there in the tin? ....

   b How many plain biscuits are there? ....

29 a How many faces are there on a triangular based pyramid? ....

b How many vertices are there on a cube? ....

c How many edges are there on a cuboid? ....

d How many flat faces are there on a cylinder? ....

30 Label the following shapes.

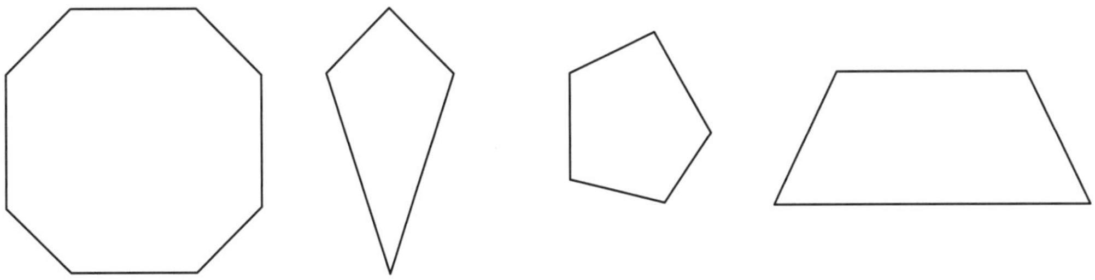

    A   B   C   D

31 Draw the following.

    a An irregular quadrilateral   **b** A scalene triangle   **c** An irregular hexagon

32

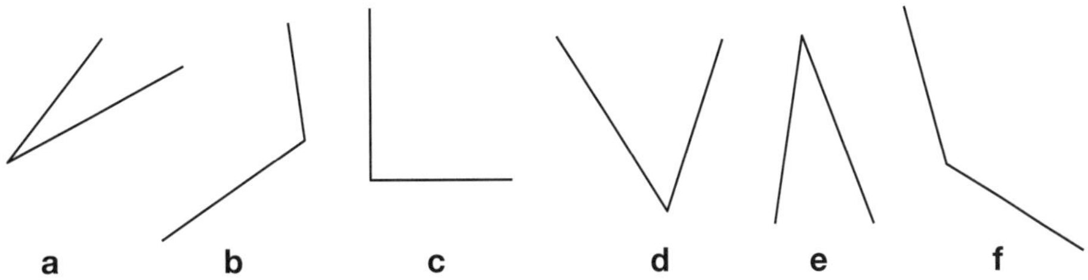

    a   b   c   d   e   f

In the angles drawn above:

    a put an X in the obtuse angles   **b** draw a square in any right angles.

33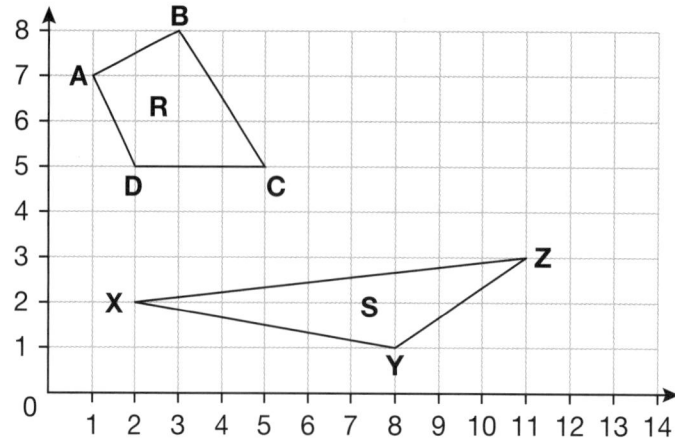

a Give the coordinates of points A, B, C and D.

A .... B .... C .... D ....

b Give the coordinates of points X, Y and Z.

X .... Y .... Z ....

c On the same grid plot the points (7,8) (10,7) (13,7) (13,5) (11,4) and (8,5), join them together and label the shape T.

d Give the special names of the shapes.

R .... S .... T ....

34 Using the grid in question 34, plot the points (6,1) and (6,8) and join them with a dotted line, and plot the points (1,3) and (14,3) and join them with a straight line.

What are the coordinates of the point where the two lines cross? ....

35 What is the perimeter of a regular octagon with sides measuring $8\frac{1}{2}$ cm? ....

36 How wide is a pool which has a perimeter of 140 m and a length of 50 m? ....

37 Box A measure 20 cm × 30 cm × 40 cm, and box B measures 20 cm × 30 cm × 30 cm.

a What is the volume of box A? ....

b What is the volume of box B? ....

c How many more cm cubes can fit into box A than into box B? ....

38 How many ml are there in the following?

   a 64 litres .... **b** 3.75 litres .... **c** 100 litres ....

39 a How many cubic mm are there in 1 cubic cm? ....

   b How many cubic cm are there in 1 cubic m? ....

	1st train	2nd train	3rd train	4th train	5th train
Station A	09:10	10:20	11:30	12:40	13:50
Station B	09:35	–	–	13:05	14:20
Station C	09:50	10:45	–	13:20	14:40
Station D	10:15	11:10	12:15	13:45	15:10

40 Tom misses the 10:20 train at station A, how long does he have to wait for the next train? ....

41 How much quicker is the journey from station A to station D on the 3rd train than on the 4th train? ....

42 Which two trains take the same amount of time to go from station A to station D?

   ....

43 How much slower is the journey from station B to station C on the 5th train than on the 4th train? ....

44

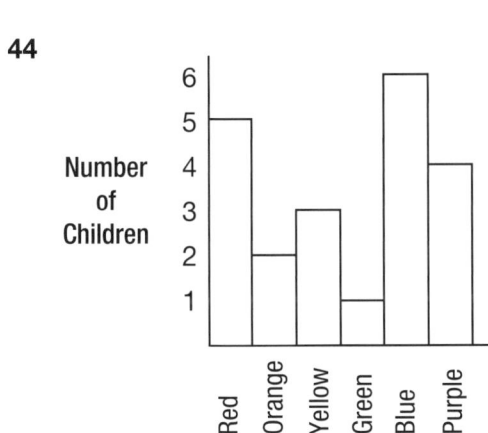

Graph to show favourite colours

   a The favourite colours of how many children are recorded in this bar graph?

   ....

   b How many more children chose purple than orange?

   ....

   c Order the colours from the least favourite to the most popular colour.

   ....

   ....

45

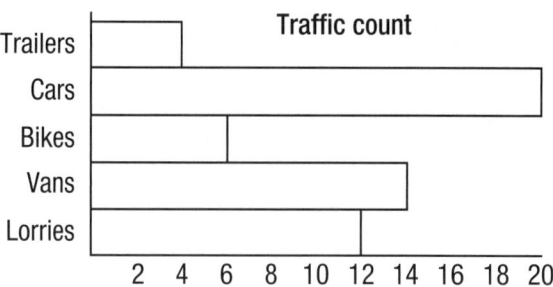

A traffic count was done on a motorway and the results are shown on this bar graph.

a How many cars were recorded? ....

b How many more vans were there than trailers? ....

c There were twice as many .... as there were ....

46

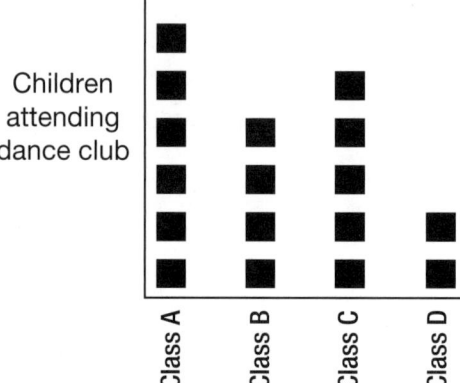

■ = 5 children

a All of class A attended dance club. How many children are in class A? ....

b There are 100 children altogether in the four classes. What fraction did not attend dance class? ....

c Half of class B have a brother or sister in class D. How many children in class B do not have a brother or sister in class D? ....

47

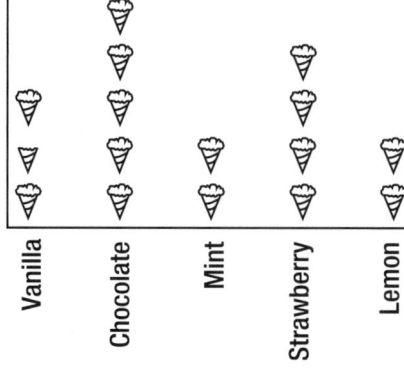

= 2 Ice creams

a How many ice creams were sold? ....

b How many more strawberry ice creams were sold than lemon? ....

c How many more of the two most popular
ice creams were sold than the two least popular? ....

48

	Speaks Spanish	Does not speak Spanish
Speaks Arabic	24	30
Does not speak Arabic	35	11

a How many children speak Spanish? ....

b How many children speak Arabic? ....

c How many more children speak both languages than neither language? ....

49 The tally chart records the results from a class of 32 children.

Plays hockey and not table tennis	ЖЖ
Plays table tennis and not hockey	Ж III
Plays hockey and table tennis	ЖЖ
Does not play hockey or table tennis	IIII

Transfer the data to the Carroll diagram below.

	Plays hockey	Does not play hockey
Plays table tennis		
Does not play table tennis		

50 Share £372.66 equally between 6 people. ....

51 308.25 × 5 = ...

Test Paper 2

1 350.4 + 1902.7 = ...

2 5040 − 379 = ...

Which pattern or shape continues or completes the sequence on the left?
Underline the answer.

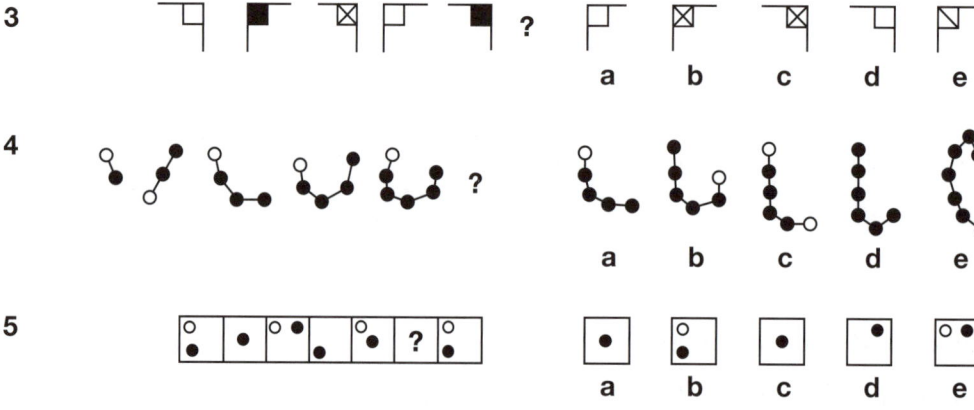

Which code matches the shape or pattern given at the end of each line?
Underline the answer.

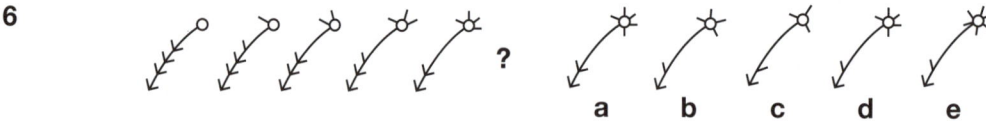

7   AX   BY   CZ   BX   ?   AY   AZ   BZ   CX   CY
                               a   b   c   d   e

8   AX   BX   AY   CX   ?   AX   BY   CY   AY   BX
                               a   b   c   d   e

9   DY   EZ   DX   FY   ?   FX   DZ   EX   EY   FX
                               a   b   c   d   e

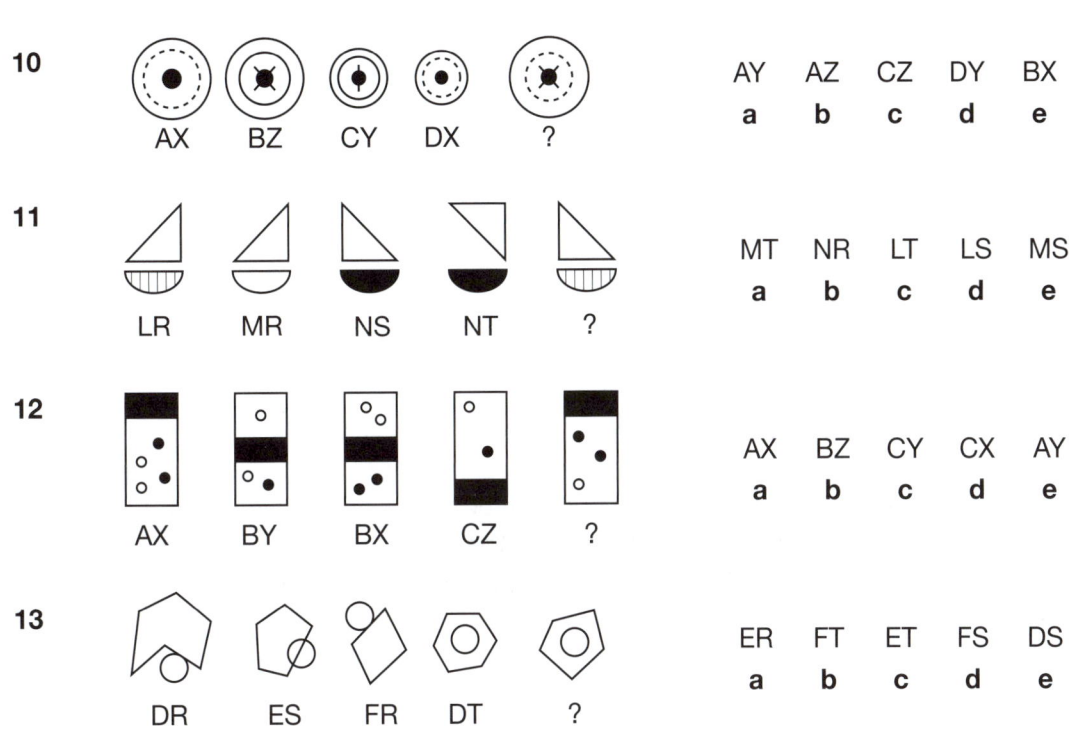

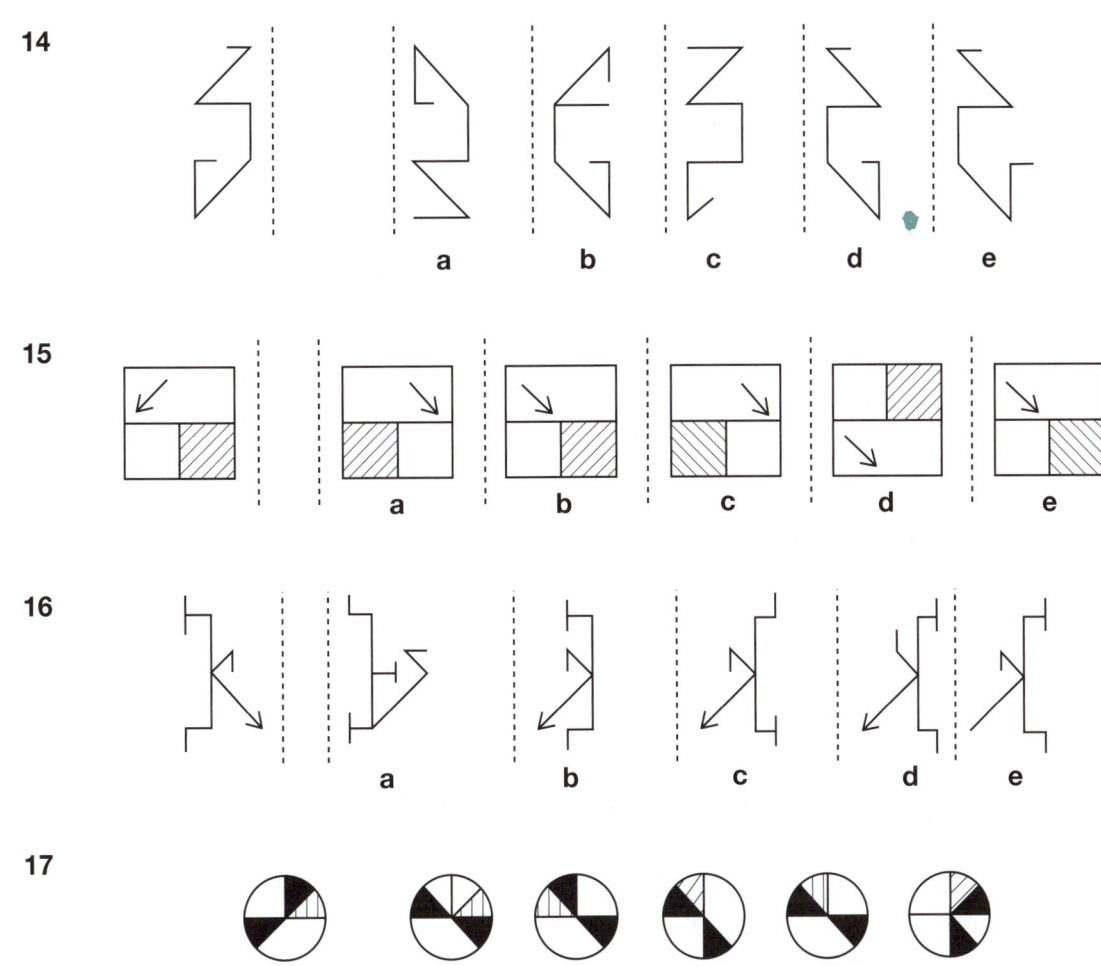

Which shape on the right is a reflection of the shape on the left? Underline the answer.

18 405.23 × 20 = ...

19 Write these fractions as decimal numbers.

$\frac{1}{2}$ .... $\frac{3}{10}$ .... $\frac{3}{4}$ ....

20 420.68 − .... = 395.77

21 What is the total of 35.7, 51.38 and 10.87? ....

22 Mrs Zahidi's food shop costs £84.55. She bought three packs of biscuits for the price of two and three yogurts for the price of two. The biscuits cost 85p a pack and the yogurts were 65p each. What would her total bill have been without the three-for-two savings?

....

23 James is taller than Ralph and Tom, Tom is shorter that Dan and Ralph. If James is the second tallest, who is the tallest?

....

24 Eggs are packed into boxes of 1 dozen. A crate can hold 20 boxes. If $\frac{1}{10}$ of the eggs in the crate arrive broken, how many eggs are broken?

....

25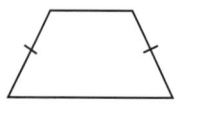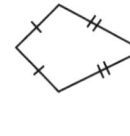

        a   **b**   **c**

Name these three shapes and draw one line of symmetry across each of them.

26 Fill in the missing words.

  a a .... is any 4-sided shape.

  b a .... has opposite sides that are parallel and equal in length

    and .... right angles.

  c a .... triangle has .... sides the same length.

27 Name the 3D shapes that will be formed from these nets.

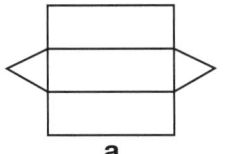  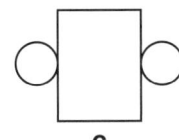 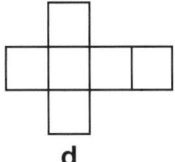

     a   b   c   d

a ....   b ....   c ....   d ....

28 Underline the angles below that are acute angles and draw a circle around those that are obtuse angles.

36°   96°   58°   134°   220°   71°   111°

29 Through how many degrees does the hour hand on a clock face rotate when it goes from 2 o'clock to 5 o'clock? ....

30

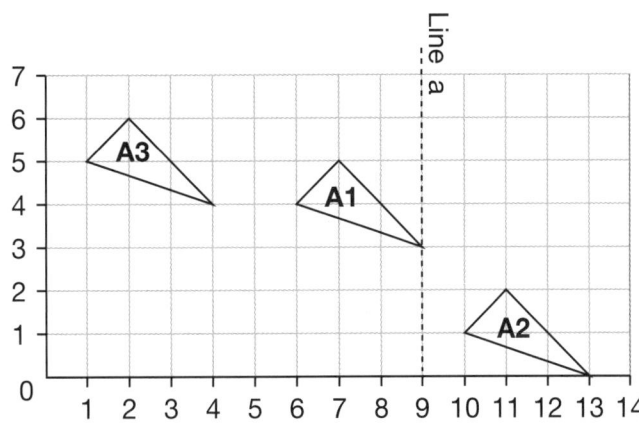

    a Describe the translation of triangle A1 to A2. ....

    b Describe the translation of A2 to A3. ....

    c Reflect triangle A1 with line a as the line of reflection, and label the reflected triangle A4.

    d Translate triangle A3 right 3 and down 3, and label the new triangle A5.

    e What are the coordinates of triangle A5? ....

31 If 1 kg is approximately 2.2 lbs, how many kg is 22 lbs? ....

32 Convert 3407.58 m to km, m and cm. ....

33 How many seconds are there in 1½ hours? ....

34 The perimeter of a regular pentagon is 124 cm. What is the length of each side?

Give your answer in mm. ....

35 If each grid square is 1 square cm, what is the area of these four shapes?

a   b   c   d

a .... b .... c .... d ....

36 If the length of a rectangle is 34 cm and its perimeter is 120 cm:

a What is its width? ....   **b** What is its area? ....

37 A bus leaves the bus station every nine minutes. The first bus leaves at 08:02.

a At what times do buses between 08:00 and 09:00 leave? ....

b How many buses leave between 08:00 and 09:00? ....

c What time does the first bus after 09:00 leave the station? ....

38 School starts at 8.55 a.m., and it takes Sam 23 minutes to walk to there.

a When must he leave home to get to school exactly on time? ....

b On Tuesday he wants to get there 15 minutes early. When must he leave home? ....

c School ends at 3.30 p.m. How long is the school day? ....

39

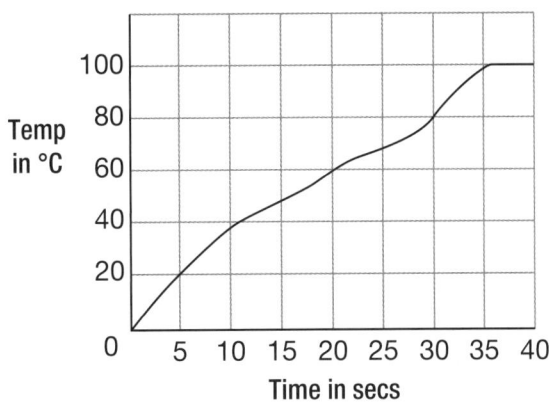

This graph shows how the temperature of some water in a heater changes with time.

a How long did it take for the water to get to 40 degrees? ....

b What temperature was it after 30 seconds? ....

c How long did it take to go from 0 degrees to 100 degrees? ....

40

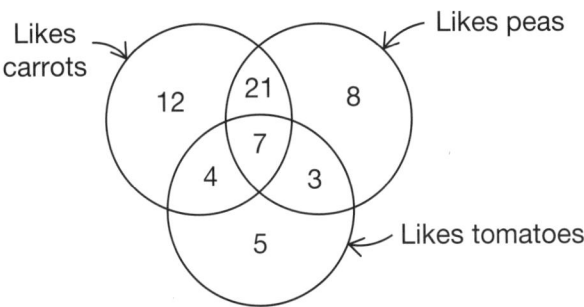

Children were offered three different vegetables. This diagram shows how many osewhich vegetables.

a How many children chose only peas? ....

b How many chose peas and carrots? ....

c How many chose carrots and tomatoes? ....

d How many children chose two of the three vegetables offered? ....

e How many chose all three vegetables? ....

f Which was the most popular vegetable? ....

41 A class of 32 children went to the library. Those that borrowed books from the library recorded what type of books they were.

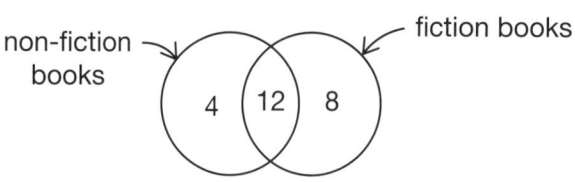

a How many children chose fiction books? ....

b How many children borrowed non-fiction books? ....

c How many children did not borrow any books from the library? ....

d What fraction of the class did borrow library books? ....

Which is the odd one out? Underline the answer.

42

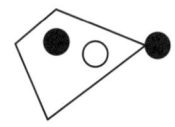  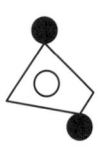 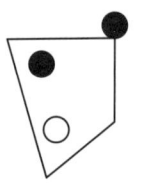 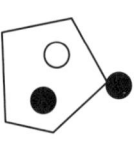

   a   b   c   d   e

43

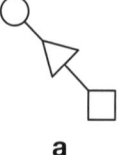 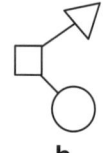 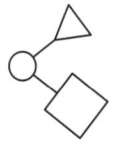 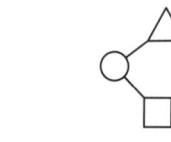

   a   b   c   d   e

44

 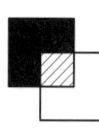   

   a   b   c   d   e

45 Complete the numbers in these number chains.

a

b

46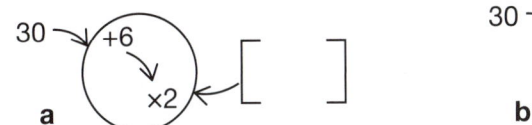

What number comes out of these function machines when the number 30 goes in?

47 What is the value of the 6 in these numbers? The first one has been done for you.

a 256.38   **6 units**

b 16 328 ....

c 34.61 ....

d 9632.42 ....

48 What number comes next in these sequences?

a 101   97   93   89   ....

b 10   11   13   16   ....

49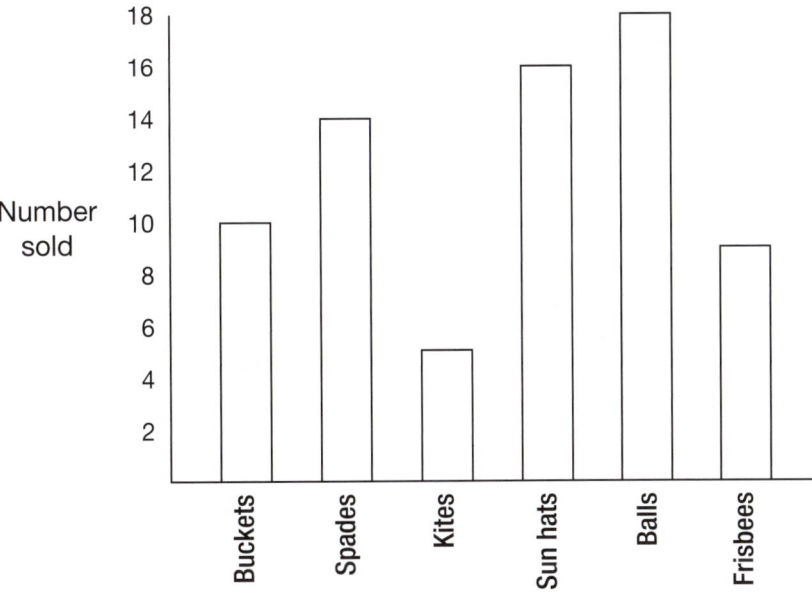

a How many more spades were sold than buckets? ....

b How many fewer kites were sold than sunhats? ....

c What was the total number of beach balls and frisbees sold? ....

d How many items were sold altogether? ....

Total 70

Keywords

Some special words and symbols are used in this book. You will find them in **bold** when they appear in the Papers. These words are explained here.

anticlockwise	movement in the opposite direction to the hands of a clock
area	the space inside a shape. Area is measured in square units, for example square centimetres (cm²) or square metres (m²)
clockwise movement	in the same direction as of the hands of a clock
coordinate	a pair of numbers used to locate a point. The first number is the
distance	along the horizontal line and the second number is the distance along the vertical line
cube	a regular 3-dimensional solid shape where every face is an identical squavre and every angle a right angle
cubic centimetre	The unit used to measure volume (also written as cm³)
cubic metre	The unit used to measure volume (also written as m³)
cuboid	a 3-dimensional solid shape where each surface is a rectangle (includes squares) and every angle is a right angle
degrees	1) the unit of measurement for temperature
	2) the unit of measurement of angle, with 360 degrees making one complete turn The symbol ° can be used instead of the word 'degrees'
difference	to find the difference between two numbers, take the smaller number away from the larger number
digit	any single number, for example 4 has one digit, 37 has two digits, 437 has three digits
equilateral triangle	a triangle which has all its sides of the same length
hexagon	a 2D shape that has 6 interior angles and 6 sides
graph	a pictorial representation or a diagram that presents data or values in an organised way
irregular shape	a shape which has sides that are different lengths
isosceles triangle	a triangle which has two sides the same length
kite	a four-sided shape with two pairs of adjoining sides the same length
mirror line	the line in which a shape can be reflected, like the reflection in a mirror

multiple	the product of a number multiplied by another number
parallel	two lines are parallel when they are an equal distance along their entire length
perimeter	the distance round the outside of a shape
pictogram	a diagram that records something using pictures
polygon	a shape with three or more sides
prism	a shape which has the same section all the way through, e.g. a 'tent' shape is a triangular prism
quadrilateral	any 2D shape with four sides and four interior angles
rectangle	a quadrilateral that has four right angles and opposite sides equal in length
regular shape	a shape which has sides that are all the same length
rotate	to turn an object clockwise or anticlockwise around a given fixed point
round	roughly or approximately, for example 42 rounded to the nearest 10 is 40, 470 rounded to the nearest 100 is 500
scalene triangle	a triangle which has sides that are all different lengths
square	a square is a rectangle with four equal sides
sum	the answer when you add two numbers together. The sum of 2 and 4 is 6
symmetry	if a shape has symmetry it has one or more mirror lines like this:

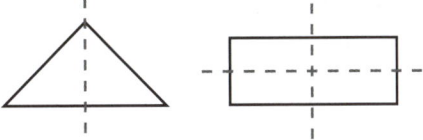

tally chart	a simple way of recording and counting frequencies, with each occurrence shown by a tally mark where every fifth tally is a horizontal line through the previous four vertical lines, making a set of five total the sum of a number of values all added together
total	the sum of a number of values all added together
Venn diagram	a chart for sorting information of different kinds
volume	The measurement of space inside an object
x axis	the name given to the horizontal line going across a graph
y axis	the name given to the vertical line going up along a graph

11+ Study Guide

Essentials

- Don't worry too much about the level that you start at. Beginning with an easier book can help your confidence.
- Make sure you have the right equipment – you will need your pencils, an eraser, and a notebook.
- This book contains skills guidance and worked examples, but if you need more help with technique, the Bond Handbooks might also be useful to you.

Studying Effectively

1 Turn to the first topic and read the Key Skills box. You might want to read it a few times or with someone else to understand it properly or to underline key words.

2 Read the worked example a few times and make sure you understand it.

3 In your notebook, write down the topic heading and the worked example on a new page. This is for you to revise and remember. Once you have completed the final book, you will have a super-useful notebook that you can use in secondary school.

4 Now set a timer – a kitchen timer, a watch or phone with an alarm – for the timed section.

5 Work your way through the questions carefully. If you don't know the answer to something, draw a circle around the question number and take your best guess. This is important as you can find patterns if you make mistakes and it highlights where you need to consolidate.

6 Ask someone to mark the paper for you or mark it yourself and see where you made mistakes. Is there a common pattern? For every mistake, decide if it is not knowing the technique properly, not consolidating the technique enough or a loss of focus and label this next to each question using T = technique, C = consolidation, F = focus.

7 Have another go at the questions you made errors in to understand what you did wrong. If it is vocabulary problem, write down the word with its meaning / synonym / antonym at the back of your book so that you widen your vocabulary range.

Making Mistakes

Everyone makes mistakes and they are an important part of how we learn. The reason we practise before an exam is so that we can make those mistakes in a safe space rather than in the test itself and that way we can learn from them and make fewer mistakes when it really matters.

Remember that there is no such thing as a 'silly mistake'. You are not silly, and neither is your mistake. It is usually not understanding the technique, not consolidating the skill needed so that it is only partially remembered, or you have lost focus. Losing focus does not mean that you have done something bad, it just means that your attention was on something else. These tips can help:

Not Understanding the Technique:

- Go back to the learning section and reread the key skills box.
- Look at the worked example that you have in your notebook.
- Use the Bond Handbook for more support.

Not Consolidating Enough:

- It is amazing how much consolidation is needed by everyone so don't worry about doing lots of additional questions.
- Look at Bond online for some more questions to help you revise.
- Ask someone to test you on the technique.

Losing Focus:

- Make sure that you are not too tired, hungry, thirsty or distracted.
- Work out where you have made a mistake and break it down into sections. It might be that you focus on tricky division, but go too fast when it comes to addition. It might be that you read the comprehension extract, but you lost focus and misread it.
- Once you have identified the problem area, make sure that in new questions, you check yourself and focus carefully.

Common Problems

'I don't have time to study.'

Make sure that you have a timetable that is doable. If you have lots of activities that take up time, perhaps break your work up. The books all have timing sections so fit in smaller sections when you can. It's important to talk to your parent if you feel that you need more time for your 11+ work.

'I find it hard to complete my homework as I want to play instead.'

Motivation is difficult for most people. Don't completely stop all fun activities during the 11+ but get a balance. Key to this is a timetable so you know when, what and where to study. Make sure it is doable and build in something fun if you complete your homework for the day. Another tip is to write down your reasons for doing the 11+. Whether it is for your own personal sense of achievement, keeping your family happy, getting into the school your friends are going to, or even that the school is just more convenient, understanding how important each of those reasons is for you and focussing on that can help you to commit the time required to make it happen. If you can't find strong enough reasons for committing the time, perhaps talk with your family about it.

'My friend is using different books to me.'

The Bond 11+ system covers English/Verbal Reasoning and Maths/Non-verbal reasoning/spatial awareness. Bond has had many decades of success in 11+ material. Many tutors will only use Bond for their pupils, and they get an exceptionally high pass rate. It doesn't mean that Bond is the only 11+ provider, so don't worry that your friend is using different material. What is important is that you are fully prepared for your CEM online exam, and you can have confidence in the Bond system.

'I'm scared of failing.'

It is natural to feel that. Remember that you cannot climb a mountain in one gigantic step. You need lots and lots of little steps to get to the top. The 11+ is like that. You can't sit down and learn everything straight away, but the little steps you take will lead you to the exam. Remember that every mistake can be identified and once you identify it, you may be able to understand it and solve the problem for next time. Mistakes are perfection in progress! If a selective school is the best learning environment for you, then you can work little and often through the books and then test papers leading up to the exam. If you find it too much and you are working at your full potential already, then maybe a school that is not selective will suit your learning better. There is no 'best school' and 'worst school' for everyone. It is the best school for an individual child. Do talk to someone about your feelings though as you need to feel supported.

'My friend has a tutor. Do I need one?'

Whether or not to have tutor depends on many different factors, including where your particular strengths and challenges lie, your own approach to learning, and whether your parents are comfortable with the costs involved. The Bond system is rigorous and aims to support every child with a range of books and learning materials. The Bond Handbooks can do the job of a tutor and many tutors also use the Bond books and Handbooks with their pupils. Bond has been providing 11+ material since the 1960s, helping thousands of pupils to pass their 11+ exams without having a tutor.

'I don't want to do the 11+ exam.'

This is a conversation to have with your family, but the best advice might be to follow the 11+ books anyway. They will teach you skills, techniques and methods that will give you self-confidence regardless of the secondary school you attend. No knowledge is a waste, and you will be keeping your options open.

There is more information on the Bond website. Bond has a Parent's Guide to the 11+ and there is a range of supportive printed and online material. See online for further details: www.bond11plus.co.uk

Bond 11+ Maths and Non-verbal Reasoning
Assessment Practice for the CEM test

8–9 Years

ANSWERS
AND PROGRESS CHART

OXFORD

Answers

Learning Paper 1: Number Skills

1 a **500** 4<u>6</u>6: 6 is greater than 5, so round the 4 hundreds up to 5 giving 500.
   b **200** 2<u>3</u>9: 3 is less than 5, so the hundreds remain unchanged giving 200.
   c **3000** 29<u>9</u>0: 9 is greater than 5, so round the 29 up giving 30 hundreds, which is 3000.
   d **3600** 35<u>8</u>1: 8 is greater than 5, so round the 5 up to 6 giving 3600.
2 a **4000** 37<u>5</u>2 7 is greater than 5, so round the 3 up to 4 giving 4000
   b **10000** 9<u>5</u>49 when the digit is 5 or more it rounds up, so the 9 rounds up to 10 giving 10 000
   c **52000** 51<u>5</u>00 when the digit is 5 or more it rounds up, so the 1 rounds up to 2 giving 52 000
   d **20 000** 19<u>9</u>59 9 is greater than 5, so the thousands are rounded up from 19 to 20 giving 20 000
3 **75** 1000 − 325 = 675; 675 − 600 = 75
4 **£2.50** £19 + £8.50 = £27.50; £30 − £27.50 = £2.50
5 a **£2.56** £1.25 + 49p + 82p = £2.56
   b **£7.44** £10 − £2.56 = £7.44
6 a **£11** 4 × £3.50 = £14; £25 − £14 = £11
   b **2** 2 × £4.99 = £9.98, with £1.02 left on the gift card, which is not enough for another book.
7 a **53** 66 − 13 = 53
   b **33** Half of 66 is 66 ÷ 2 = 33
   c **20** White = total minus the blue and minus the red = 66 − 33 − 13 = 20
8 This type of question doesn't have to be completed in order, so begin with the easiest equations first.
   a **2** 15 − 13 = 2
   b **7** 13 − 6 = 7
   c **−** 7 − 1 = 6
   d **6** 7 − 1 = 6
   e **3** 2 + 1 = 3
   f **9** 6 + 3 = 9

13	+	2	=	15
−		+		−
7	−	1	=	6
=		=		=
6	+	3	=	9

9 **120** 4 × 3 = 12; 12 × 10 = 120
10 **£40** 360 ÷ 9 = 40
11 **3000** 30 × 50 = 1500; 2 × 1500 = 3000
    You could also remove the zeros to simplify the sum: 3 × 5 = 15 therefore 30 × 50 = 1500; ? ÷ 2 = 1500 so complete the inverse to find the answer: 2 × 1500 = 3000
12 <u>360</u>   <u>471</u>   23   35   <u>150</u>   41   <u>81</u>
    These can be divided exactly by 3.
13 a **30** 240 ÷ 8 = 30
    b **59** 2 × 62 = 124; 124 + 57 = 181; 240 − 181 = 59
14 a **6** 3 × 6 = 18; 24 − 18 = 6
    b **30** 6 × 5 = 30
    c $\frac{1}{4}$ (a quarter)
15 a **6 kg** 3 kg × 2 = 6 kg
    b **1500 ml** (or **1$\frac{1}{2}$ litres**) 500 ml × 3 = 1500 ml which is 1$\frac{1}{2}$ litres.
    c **12 jars** 6 kg of sugar × 2 jars per kg = 12

Learning Paper 2: Sequences

1 **14, 44, 88** 42 ÷ 3 = 14; 14 + 30 = 44; 44 × 2 = 88
2 **14** The difference between each number is 8 and the numbers get smaller so it is subtracted (22 − 8 = 14)
3 a **28, 32** The difference is 4 and the numbers get bigger so it is added (24 + 4 = 28 and 28 + 4 = 32)
   b **40, 32** The difference is 8 and the numbers get smaller so it is subtracted (48 − 8 = 40 and 40 − 8 = 32)
   c **299, 269** The difference is 10 and the numbers get smaller so it is subtracted (309 − 10 = 299 and 279 − 10 = 269)
   d **66, 56** The difference is 5 and the numbers get smaller so it is subtracted (7 − 5 = 66 and 61 − 5 = 56)
4 **124** The difference is 5 and the numbers get bigger so it is added (119 + 5 = 124)
5 a **76** Work back through the 'machine' doing the inverse operations: 43 × 2 = 86; 86 − 10 = 76
   b **44** 27 × 2 = 54; 54 − 10 = 44
6 **e** The first five shapes are repeated along the sequence.
7 **d** The short line moves progressively down and along the lines of the L-shape.
8 **a** The number of straight lines in the 'coil' pattern increases by one each time.
9 **e** The amount of 'sand' in the lower bulb of the timer increases along the sequence.
10 **c** The zigzag line always starts at the bottom, and the number of lines in the pattern increases by one each time.
11 **e** The number of short diagonal lines projecting from the vertical line increases by one each time, projecting alternately to the left and to the right moving up the vertical.
12 **c** The short line moves in a clockwise direction away from the long line which remains horizontal, and there is a black spot at the end of both lines.
13 **b** The shading of the square follows a repeating pattern of diagonal lines, white, grey, and the circle alternates between white and black.
14 **a** The shapes follow a pattern of circle, triangle, square with three large ones followed by three small ones, and the shading alternates between diagonal lines and white.
15 **d** A white circle or a joining straight line are added alternately to the pattern along the sequence.
16 **b** The angular line pattern increases by two lines each time, with each pattern starting in the lower left position.

17 **a** The position of the triangle on the side of the square rotates 90 degrees clockwise along the sequence, and the triangle is always separated from the square by a dotted line.

18 **a** The circle moves anticlockwise around the inner angles of the triangle, and from the answer options given it can be worked out that the three triangles with black circles will be followed by three triangles with white circles.

Learning Paper 3: Number Skills and Pattern Completion

1 **a** **30** $\frac{1}{4}$ of 80 is 80 ÷ 4 which is 20 so 20 orange + 20 lemon + 10 blackberry = 50; 80 − 50 = 30 apple

b $\frac{1}{2}$ 20 orange + 20 lemon = 40; 40/80 can be simplified to $\frac{1}{2}$

c **2 orange, 2 lemon, 1 blackberry, 3 apple**
20 orange ÷ 10 = 2; 20 lemon ÷ 10 = 2; 10 blackberry ÷ 10 = 1; 30 apple ÷ 10 = 3

2 **$10\frac{1}{2}$** $4\frac{1}{2}$ 6 $7\frac{1}{2}$ 9

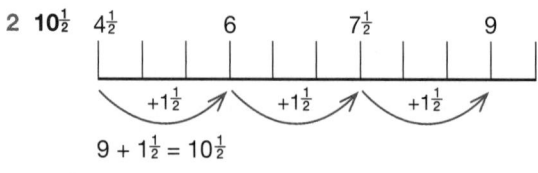

$9 + 1\frac{1}{2} = 10\frac{1}{2}$

3 **a** $\frac{2}{3}$

b $\frac{2}{6}$

c $\frac{3}{5}$

d $\frac{1}{4}$

4 Count the number of squares to find the denominator. Look at the denominator in the fraction shown and decide what it has been multiplied by to get the same number. Then multiply the numerator by this number also.

a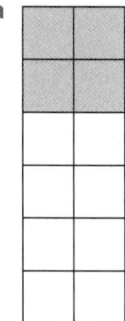

(Any 4 squares)

b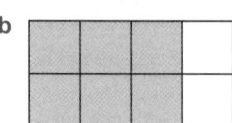

(Any 6 squares)

c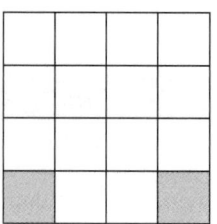

(Any 2 squares)

5 Work out the easiest fractions first. Find which number the other numerators or denominators have been multiplied or divided by. Then multiply or divide the other number in the fraction by the same.

a $\frac{3}{6} = \frac{2}{4} = \frac{4}{8}$
All these fractions are equivalent of $\frac{1}{2}$

b $\frac{2}{10} = \frac{20}{100} = \frac{1}{5}$

c $\frac{6}{8} = \frac{3}{4} = \frac{30}{40}$

6 Lines should link $\frac{1}{2}$ to $\frac{6}{12}$; $\frac{3}{4}$ to $\frac{75}{100}$; $\frac{7}{10}$ to **0.7**; $\frac{1}{4}$ to **0.25**

7 **a** **402.04**
b **702,072.7**

8 **0.01 < 0.1 < 10.01 < 10.1 < 100 < 100.1**

9 **100** 1.42 × 100 = 142 as the decimal point moves 2 places to the right when multiplying by 100.

10 **4.58 < 4.59 < 4.84 < 5.01 < 5.10**

11 **b** All of the shapes on the left have three straight lines with two right angles between them, and the shapes are completed with a curvy line.

12 **c** All of the shapes on the left have a plain line which extends into the white triangle that forms the arrowhead.

13 **e** All of the shapes on the left are parts of a circle.

14 **d** All of the shapes on the left are triangles with a circle going over one of the vertices (corners).

15 **a** All of the 'house' shapes on the left have a trapezium shape for the roof, one window and one door.

16 **c** The patterns on the left have five elements.

17 **d** All of the shapes on the left have two straight lines joined by one curvy line, with a circle in the middle of the shape.

18 **b** All of the shapes on the left are made up of four squares in a Z-shape, and the two squares that are adjacent to two other squares have black spots in them.

19 **c** All of the shapes on the left are rectangles with a white circle, a black circle and an x inside them.

20 **c** All of the shapes on the left are circles with a double outline, and with the central circle divided into eight sections.

Learning Paper 4: Logic and Codes

1. **d** The first letter represents the number of circles in the shape (A is 3, B is 2, C is 1); the second letter represents the orientation of the line (M is horizontal, N is vertical).
2. **a** The first letter represents the style of the fish shape (A wide plain body, B long plain body, C wide patterned body); the second letter represents the direction that the 'fish' is facing (L is left, R is right).
3. **b** The first letter represents the number of cherries (A is 1, B is 2, C is 3); the second letter represents the pattern where the cherry stalks meet (X is a line, Y is a black spot).
4. **e** The first letter represents the triangles on the shape (A has 2, B has none); the second letter represents the pattern of the oval shape (X is plain, Y is spotted, Z has vertical lines).
5. **b** The first letter represents the shape of the lolly (A is a single curve, wide shape, B is a long cylindrical shape, C is a double curved wide shape); the second letter represents the shading (X is white, Y is grey, Z is diagonal line shading).
6. **b** The first letter represents the number of lines (A is 3, B is 4, C is 5); the second letter represents the shading of the circle (X is black, Y is white).
7. **a** The first letter indicates the position of the vertical line coming down from the horizontal line (L is at the left end, M is in the middle, R is at the right end); the second letter indicates the horizontal line styles (A has two plain lines, B has one plain and one dotted line, C has two dotted lines).
8. **c** The first letter represents the fraction of the square shaded grey (A is a quarter, B is a half, C is three-quarters); the second letter represents the shading of the other part of the square (H is horizontal lines, V is vertical lines).
9. **b** The first letter represents the shading of the central square (A is black, B is lined, C is white); the second letter represents the position of the short lines on the octagon (X has the lines crossing the diagonal sides of the octagon, Y has the short lines crossing the horizontal and vertical sides of the octagon).
10. **a** The first letter represents the mouth of the snake (A has no tongue, B has a forked tongue in the mouth); the second letter represents the pattern of the body (X is white, Y is black and white, Z has a zigzag pattern).
11. **d** The first letter represents the shading of the shape (D has horizontal lines, E has grid lines, F is grey); the second letter represents the curved line along the top of the shape (S has two shallow curves at the top, T has two deeper curves along the top).
12. a **10 cm** 3.30 to 5.30 is 2 hours, 2 × 1 cm = 2 cm
    b **5 hours** At 1 cm an hour, it will take 5 hours to burn 5 cm of the candle.
    c **9.30 p.m.** The candle has to burn 6 cm to reach 6 cm tall, and that will take 6 hours, 6 hours after 3.30 p.m. is 9.30 p.m.
13. **Tom** Asim can be second or third, Tom can be first or second. If Hani did better than Tom, then Tom is second.
14. **Tim** Add the names in the correct place according to the information given:
    oldest Tim Sol? Amal Sol? Ben *youngest*
15. a **Taya**
    b **Julie**
    c

	Likes dogs		Does not like dogs	
Likes cats	Julie	Aman	Taya	Ben
Does not like cats	Ted	Bill	Ray	Asher

16. **10** Marks on day 1 + marks on day 2 is 7 + 9 = 16, 46 − 16 = 30, so must have got 10 marks on the other days.
17. a **20** Along the row for grey socks it shows 20 pairs of socks are washed each day, therefore there are 20 boys.
    b **Tue, Wed, Sat**. Only these days show 20 socks washed.
18. a **120 cm** (or 1.2 m). 12 steps × 10 cm = 120 cm
    b **30 cm** 80 cm − 50 cm = 30 cm
    c **40 cm** 70 cm − 30 cm = 40 cm

Learning Paper 5: Shape, Space and Grids

1. **2 circles** The cylinder has a circle at each end.
2.

Shape	Number of angles	Must it have right angles?	Number of sides
Rectangle	4	Yes	4
Octagon	8	No	8
Triangle	3	No*	3
Hexagon	6	No	6

*Although some do have a right angle, they do not have to have one to be a triangle.

3. Any shape drawn with four sides and one right angle, e.g.:

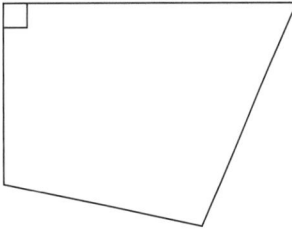

4. Tick inside angle **a** and angle **d**.
5. **6, 12, 8**
6. **d**

7. **a**

8 c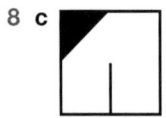

9 e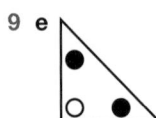

10 b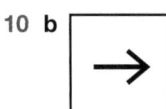

11 b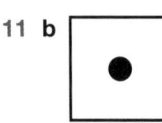

12 e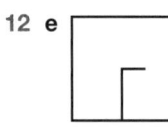

13 d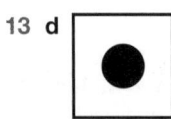

14 a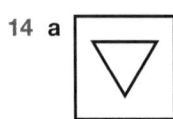

15 d

16 b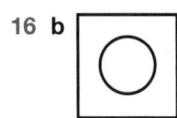

17 West

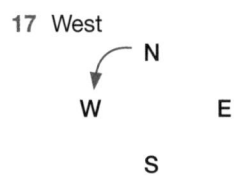

18 **180 degrees** From pointing at the 6 to pointing at the 12, the hand moves through half of a circle, $\frac{1}{2} \times 360 = 180$

19 **72 degrees** The whole pizza is 360 degrees, 360 ÷ 5 = 72 so 72 degrees for each slice. See page 10 for short division.

20 **540 degrees** One rotation is 360 degrees, half a rotation is 180, 360 + 180 = 540

21 **270 degrees** 90 × 3 = 270

22 **South** 135 degrees is one right angle (90 degrees) and half a right angle (45 degrees); 45 degrees clockwise from NE goes to E, 90 degrees clockwise from E will point to S.

23 **4** A right angle is 90 degrees, 4 × 90 = 360

24 **East** Facing west and turning left will face south, facing south and turning left again will face east.

Learning Paper 6: Position and Direction

1 A **(1,1)** B **(3,6)** C **(6,3)**
2 A **(2,3)** B **(6,6)** C **(12,4)** D **(8,1)**
3 X **(1,5)** Y **(5,25)** Notice the scale on the axes is different, so you need to read the numbers carefully.
AB and XY cross at (4,20)
4
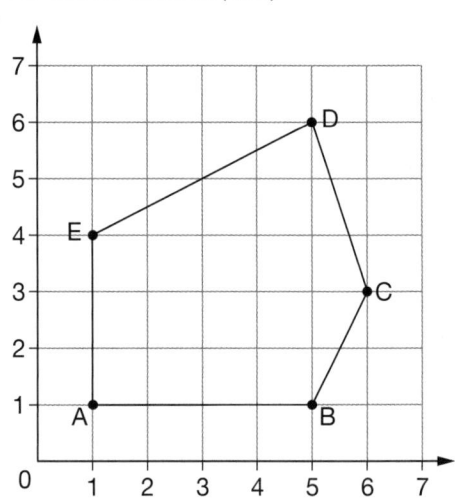

Pentagon

5
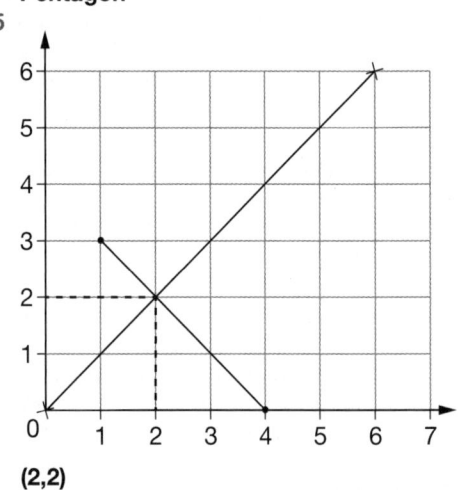

(2,2)

6 **(1,3)** If A is (1, 1) then the scale increases by 1 every two squares along the grid and every two squares up the grid.

7 (1,3) **(1,4)** (3,3) (4,3) **(4,4)** (3,5) **(5,4)** (5,6) The number on the y axis is the same for any point on a horizontal line.

8 **(8,3)**

9
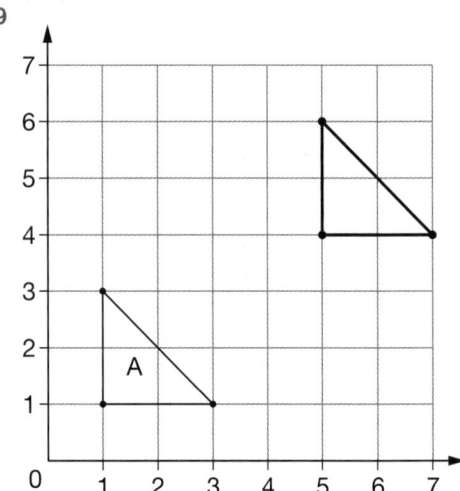

10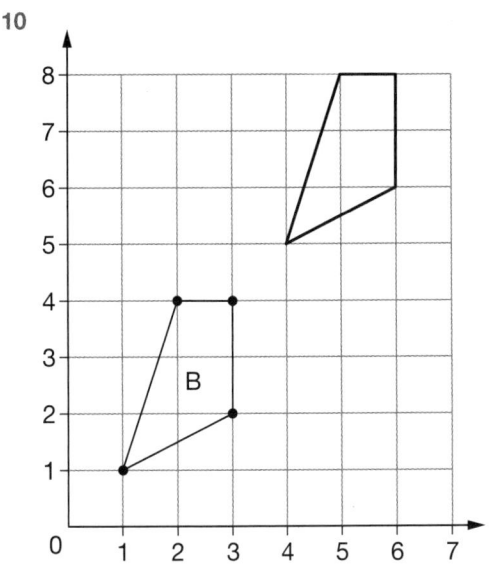

11 The scale increases in 2s, so it moves 1 square left and 2 squares down.

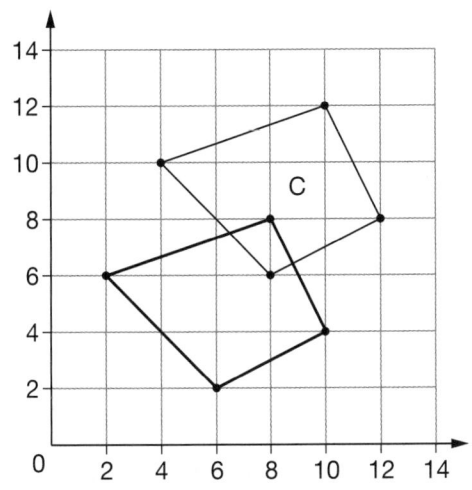

12 A to A' **(Right 4, Down 2)**
13 B to B' **(Left 2, Up 4)**
14 C to C' **(Left 5, Up 0)** or **(Left 5, Down 0)**
15 D to D' **(Right 3, Up 4)**
16 c
17 c
18 c

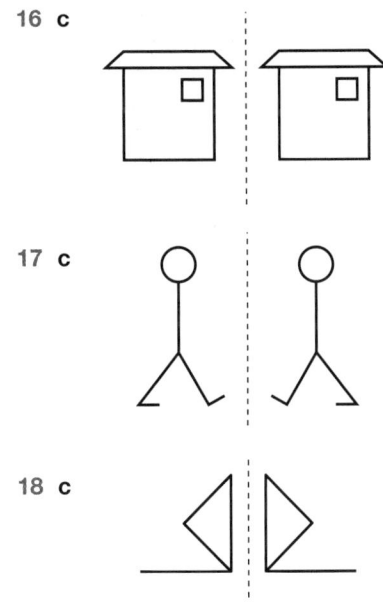

19 b
20 e
21 a
22 b
23 a
24 e

Learning Paper 7: Measurement and Pairs

1 a **18 cm** 2 p.m. to 6 p.m. is 4 hours, 4 lots of $\frac{1}{2}$ cm = 2 cm, 20 cm − 2 cm = 18 cm
   b **10 hours** as 1 cm takes 2 hours to burn.
   c **10 p.m.** 4 cm takes 8 hours, 2 p.m. plus 8 hours is 10 p.m.
2 1250 ml > 1.2 litres > 0.55 litres > 500 ml > 250 ml (It is easiest to compare when all measurements are converted to ml.)
3 a **2000 m** 1 km = 1000 m, so 2 km = 2000 m
   b **5 m** 1000 mm = 1 m, so 5000 mm = 5 m
   c **3.5 m** 100 cm = 1 m, so 350 cm = 3.5 m
   d **40 m** 1 km = 1000 m, so 0.04 km = 40 m
4 a **2 kg onions** There are 3 times as many apples as onions, so divide 6 kg apples by 3 to find 2 kg onions.
   b **600 ml vinegar** 100 ml for each kg of apples, so 6 × 100 = 600
   c **8 jars** There are 6 kg apples and $1\frac{1}{2}$ kg gives 2 jars; 4 lots of $1\frac{1}{2}$ = 6 and 4 × 2 jars = 8
5 **15 sq m** The lawn is 7 m − 2 m long and 5 m − 2 m wide, so the area is 5 × 3 = 15 sq m
6 **46 cm** The perimeter is 7 + 7 + 16 + 16 = 46 cm
7 **18 cm** 4.5 cm × 4 = 18 cm
8 a **4.4 m** (or **440 cm**) 100 + 100 + 120 + 120 = 440 cm, or 4.4 m
   b **4.8 m** (or **480 cm**) 100 + 5 + 5 = 110 and 120 + 5 + 5 = 130; so 110 + 110 + 130 + 130 = 480 cm, or 4.8 m

9 **18 bottles** 1 litre fills 4 250 ml bottles, so 4 litres fills 16 bottles, and $\frac{1}{2}$ litre fills 2 bottles. So the total is 16 + 2 = 18
10 **40 000 cm cubes** Volume is 50 × 40 × 20 = 2000 × 20 = 40 000 cm cubes. You can simplify the sum by removing the same amount of zeros from each number: 5 × 4 = 20 so 50 × 40 = 2000; 200 × 2 = 400, so 2000 × 20 = 40 000 cm cubes
11 **1000 cubes** 10 × 10 × 10 = 1000 cubes
12 **35 minutes** 15 mins from 10.45 to 11.00, and then another 20 minutes to 11.20, so 15 + 20 = 35 minutes
13 **11:06, 11:28**
14 **75 minutes** 1 hour is 60 mins, $\frac{1}{4}$ hour is 15 mins, 60 + 15 = 75 minutes
15 **1 hour 13 minutes 30 seconds** 60 mins gives 1 hour, $13\frac{1}{2}$ mins gives 13 full mins, $\frac{1}{2}$ min is 30 secs.
16 a **8 a.m.** (on Thursday)
   b **Tuesday** 6 p.m.
   c **Thursday** Mon 8h, Tue 8h, Wed 4h, Thu 9h, Fri 8h, Sat 3h.
   d **40 hours** 8h + 8h + 4h + 9h + 8h + 3h = 40h
17 **a** The second shape is the same as the first shape, with the black spots white and the white spots black.
18 **c** The number of lines in the first shape gives the number of black adjacent diamond shapes in the second shape.
19 **a** The second shape is the same as the first shape with the horizontal shading lines changed to vertical shading lines.
20 **d** The second shape is the first shape reflected in a vertical mirror line.
21 **e** The second shape has the crosses replaced with the same number of circles in the same orientation.
22 **d** The second shape is the first shape reflected in a horizontal mirror line.
23 **b** The second shape has the two parts of the first shape brought together, with the small shape resting on the line.
24 **c** The second shape is the first shape reflected in a vertical mirror line.
25 **e** The second shape is the first shape reflected in a vertical mirror line.

Learning Paper 8: Statistics and Pattern Recognition

1 Look at the number each bar is level with to find the amount of children who chose each fruit.
   a **bananas** The highest bar shows 24 for bananas.
   b **mangoes** The lowest bar shows 11 for mangoes.
   c **20**
   d **3** 18 − 15 = 3
2 a **9 mm** Between every 5 mm, the graph is separated into 5 further lines, so each horizontal line represents 1 mm.
   b **Week 3**
   c **37 mm** 9 + 13 + 5 + 10 = 37 mm

3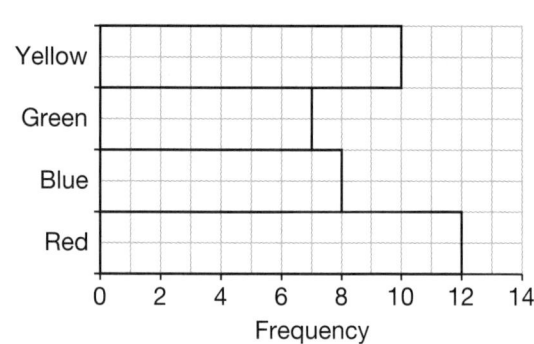

4 a **5 cm**
   b **5 weeks**
5 a **5**
   b **2**
   c **7**
   d **3**
   e **4**
   f **6**
6 a **14 goals**
   b **7 goals** 13 − 6 = 7
   c **1 goal** 10 − 9 = 1
7 a **30** Between every 5 mm, the graph is separated into 5 further lines, so each horizontal line represents 1 mm.
   b **4** 5 − 1 = 4
   c **February and May** There are five in each.
8

	Square	Not square	Total
Red	14	32	46
Not red	26	28	54
Total	40	60	100

   a **60**
   b **46**
   c **100**
9 **d** All of the shapes except d have four sides, with a triangle in the middle and a black circle outside one of the corners.
10 **b** All of the shapes except b have the arrows pointing to the bottom left corner of the page.
11 **d** All of the shapes except d are made up of three lines.
12 **d** All of the shapes except d have the arrow crossing the square from side to side.
13 **b** All of the shapes except b have one arrow pointing into the triangle and one pointing out of it.
14 **d** All of the shapes except d are made up of two circles.
15 **b** All of the shapes except b are facing the same direction.

Curveball Questions 1

1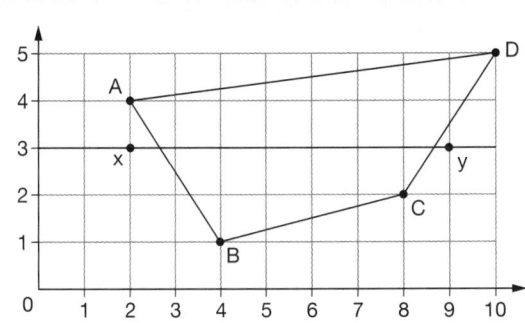

Any one of **(3,4) (4,4) (5,4) (6,4) (7,4) (8,4) (9,4)**

2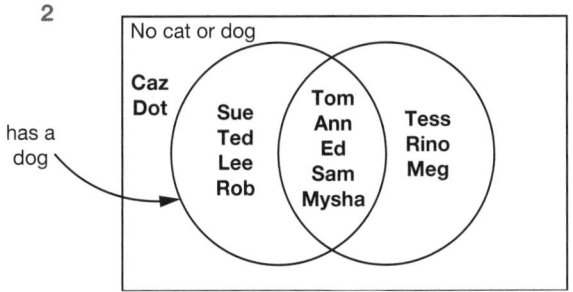

3

Mixed Paper 1

1 **4269**
2 **15** 8 + 4 + 3 = 15
3 **12, 6, 38** 4 × 3 = 12; 12 ÷ 2 = 6; 6 + 32 = 38
4 Complete the inverse to find the answer.
   a **321** 722 − 401 = 321
   b **1000** 455 + 545 = 1000
   c **6** 6 × 12 = 72
   d **100** 35 200 ÷ 100 = 352
5 **103** 752 − 649 = 103
6 **2260** 4520 ÷ 2 = 2260. See page 10 for short division.
7 **$\frac{7}{8}$** Find equivalents with the same denominator ($\frac{1}{2} = \frac{4}{8}$ and $\frac{1}{4} = \frac{2}{8}$); then add the numerators only: 4 + 2 + 1 = 7 therefore the answer is $\frac{7}{8}$
8 **35** 17 × 2 = 34, plus another $\frac{1}{2}$ gives 35 halves.

9 $\frac{6}{9}$ $\frac{1}{2}$ $\frac{2}{3}$ $\frac{4}{12}$ $\frac{5}{12}$ $\frac{20}{30}$

10 **15.4** 320 − 304.6 = 15.4
11 **8.0** The numbers are increasing by 0.4 each time, so 7.6 + 0.4 = 8.0
12 **167** 3 × 9 = 27; 7 × 20 = 140; 27 + 140 = 167
13 **21 250** 4250 × 5 can be broken down into 4000 × 5 = 20 000; 250 × 5 = 1250; 20 000 + 1250 = 21 250
14 **3** Each digit, apart from the zeros, has been multiplied by 3
15 a **1731.9** When doing the addition keep the decimal points in line:

```
    4   0   9  .  3
            3     7
1   2   8   5  .  6
─────────────────────
1   7   3   1  .  9
    1   2
```

   b **4657** When the number at the top is less than the number you are subtracting, borrow from the number at the top of the next column. If the number in the next column is a zero, change it to a 9 and borrow from the column before it.

```
        8  10
    4   7   9   15
            1   4   8
────────────────────
    4   6   5   7
```

16 **d** The first letter represents the style of arrowhead (A is black, B is curled, C is white); the second letter represents the number of black circles (X is 3, Y is 1, Z is 2).
17 **c** The first letter represents the style of shading (A is diagonal lines, B is black, C is cross-hatch lines); the second letter represents the shape of the parts in the circle (D has one line across the circle not going through the middle, E has the dividing line through the centre, F has two lines giving a 'piece of pizza' shape (also known as a 'sector')).
18 **e** The first letter represents the orientation of the U-shape (D has the shape facing right like a letter 'C', E has the U-shape upside down, F has the U-shape as a U); the second letter represents the number of short lines across the U (X has 1, Y has 2, Z has 3).
19 **e** The first letter represents the number of circles (A is 3, B is 4, C is 5); the second letter represents the number of short lines at the base (X is 1, Y is 2, Z is 3).
20 **300 books** Total length of shelving is 5 × 2 m = 10 m; 6 books take up 20 cm, 5 × 20 cm = 1 m, so 1 m takes 5 × 6 books = 30 books; there are 10 m in total, so the total books is 30 × 10 = 300
21 **Newsagent** Using initial letters for each shop a diagram can be built up from the information given:
F&C   GG (4 doors from H)   N   B   T   H
                                                (end of street)

22 **42** ½ of 24 = 12 iced buns and ¼ of 24 = 6 eclairs; 24 + 12 + 6 = 42
23 **e**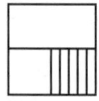
24 **e**
25 **c**
26 **c**
27 **d** All of the shapes except d have horizontal shading lines.
28 **d** All of the shapes except d have right angle triangles.
29 **c** All of the shapes except c have five short lines at the end of the longer straight line.
30 **e** All of the shapes except e have the white circle on the outer line.
31 **b** All of the shapes except b have the two lines forming an acute angle.
32 **36 cm** The perimeter is 13 + 13 + 5 + 5 = 36
33 **175 m** 50 m × 2 = 100 m, 450 m − 100 m = 350 m, 350 m ÷ 2 = 175 m
34 **24 sq m** Subtract the measurements shown to find the missing ones: 7 − 3 = 4 and 4 − 3 = 1; then separate the shape into 2 rectangles and find the area of each (7 × 3 = 21 and 3 × 1 = 3); add the answers together to find the total area (21 + 3 = 24)
35 **26 slabs** 4 × 5 = 20 so the patio needs 20 slabs; 1 × 6 = 6 so the path needs 6 slabs; 20 + 6 = 26
36 a **36** 4 × 9 = 36
   b **12** 7 × 4 = 28 on Sunday and 4 × 4 = 16 on Thursday; 28 − 16 = 12
   c **104** 4 × 26 = 104

Mixed Paper 2

1 **236**
2 **11** 67 + 22 = 89, 100 − 89 = 11
3 **305** 673 + 22 = 695, 1000 − 695 = 305
4 **470, 290** 740 650 560
   560 − 90 = **470** 380 380 − 90 = **290**
   −90 90 −90 −90 −90
5 **50, 57**
   22 29 36 43 43 + 7 = **50** 50 + 7 = **57**
   +7 +7 +7 +7 +7
6 **46.4, 48.2**
   43.7 44.6 45.5 45.5 + 0.9 = **46.4** 47.3 47.3 + 0.9 = **48.2**
   +0.9 +0.9 +0.9 +0.9 +0.9
7 **24 1 2 6 24 120 720 5040**
   1 × 2 2 × 3 6 × 4 24 × 5 120 × 6 720 × 7

8 **e** All of the shapes on the left have an oval overlapping with a circle and two lines crossing the circle edge.
9 **c** All of the shapes on the left have a triangle with a circle on the outside touching one corner, one of the shapes is black and one has diagonal line shading.
10 **d** All of the shapes on the left have two short diagonal lines from an end of the straight line.
11 **e** All of the shapes on the left have four lines coming out from a black circle.
12 **d** The first letter represents the location of the triangle in relation to the square (A is beneath the square, B is above and sloping up from bottom left to top right, C is above and sloping from top left to bottom right); the second letter represents the shape inside the square (L is a circle, M is a triangle, N is an X).
13 **c** The first letter represents the number of lines in the zigzag (D is 3, E is 4, F is 2); the second letter represents the number of short lines crossing the zigzag (X is 2, Y is 1, Z is 3).
14 **e** The first letter represents the number of white circles in the pattern (A is 3, B is 2, C is 1); the second letter represents the number of black circles (X is 1, Y is 2, Z is 3).
15 **b** The first letter represents the arrow pattern (L pointing in, M pointing out, N double-headed arrow); the second letter represents the total number of circles (X is 2, Y is 3, Z is 4).
16 **b, c and d**
17 a **6**, b **12**, c **8**
18 a **square**
   b **hexagon**
   c **parallelogram** (accept rhombus or diamond)
   d **pentagon**
19 **b, c, d and e** all have lines of symmetry. b – any line across the circle must pass through the centre; c – the line must go from the top corner to the bottom corner; d – a line may be from any corner to the corner directly opposite, or from the halfway point on any side to the half way point on the side directly opposite; e – the line may be a midline across the rectangle vertically or the midline along the rectangle horizontally.
20 a **A (3,2) B (1,7)**
   b
   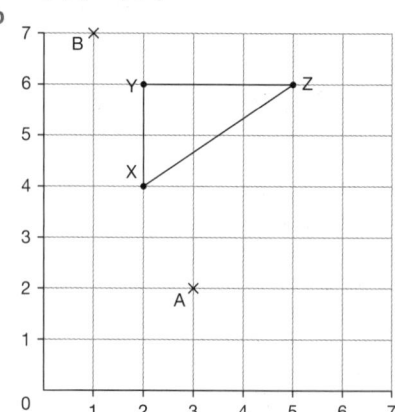
   c **Right-angled triangle**

21 (6,2)
22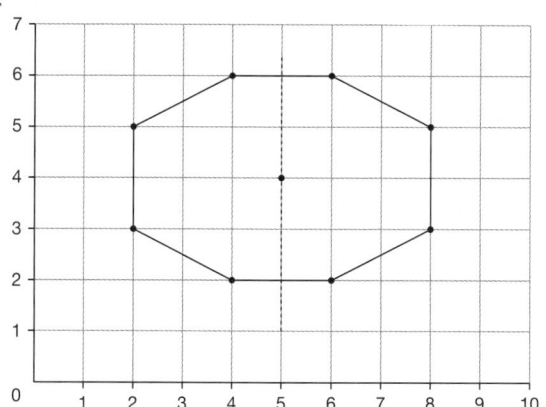
  a (5,4)
  b (5,3) (5,5) (Accept any coordinate that has 5 for the *x* axis)
23 d The second shape has the inner shape moved to the outer lower left corner of the square and the shading styles are reversed.
24 e The second shape has the square U-shape changed into a curved U-shape and the inner square changed to a circle.
25 a The second shape has the U-shape completed as a square with a black spot on the corner that had the arrow head in the first shape.
26 a The second shape is a square just the right size for the X in the first shape to form its diagonal lines.
27 d The second shape has a diagonal line drawn from the bottom left to the top right with the right-hand side shaded.
28 a 4 just white.
   b 2 red and blue.
   c 3 have red, white and blue.
   d 12 packs of just one colour.
     3 red + 5 blue + 4 white = 12
   e 11 packs with some blue.
     5 + 2 + 3 = 1 = 11
   f 7 2 (red and blue) + 1 (blue and white) + 4 (red and white) = 7
29 a $\frac{1}{4}$ 2 out of 8 are shaded giving $\frac{2}{8}$ and this simplifies to $\frac{1}{4}$

   b $\frac{5}{9}$ This fraction cannot be simplified further.

   c $\frac{1}{6}$ This fraction cannot be simplified further.

   d $\frac{1}{5}$ 2 out on 10 are shaded giving $\frac{2}{10}$ and this simplifies to $\frac{1}{5}$

30 $37\frac{1}{2}$
31 $4\frac{1}{2}$ $3\frac{1}{2} + 5\frac{1}{2} + 4 = 13$, $17\frac{1}{2} - 13 = 4\frac{1}{2}$
32 a 36
   b pizza 14 + 10 + 8 + 4 = 36
   c $\frac{1}{3}$ 8 + 4 = 12 out of 36 and $\frac{12}{36} = \frac{1}{3}$

Mixed Paper 3

1 **85** 1021 + 350 = 1371, 1456 − 1371 = 85
2 **115** 475 − 360 = 115
3 a **16** 8 + 8 = 16
  b **2** 7 − 5 = 2
4 a **7 420 133.5**
  b **2304.67**
5 d The vertical line moves down through the horizontal line, and alternates between a thick line and a thin line.
6 e The circles alternate from top to bottom of the rectangles, following a repeating pattern of black − diagonal line top left to bottom right, diagonal line top right to bottom left; the L-shape also alternates from bottom half to top half of the rectangles rotating clockwise by one right angle each time.
7 e The number of lines at the end of the shape decreases by one each time and the circle alternates between black and white.
8 b The curved line alternates between having three and two crosses on it; the total number of circles increases by one each time.
9 a

10 c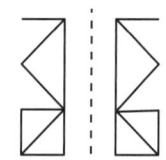

11 e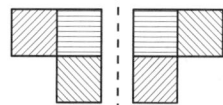

12 e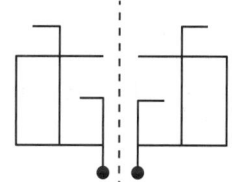

13 e

14 c

15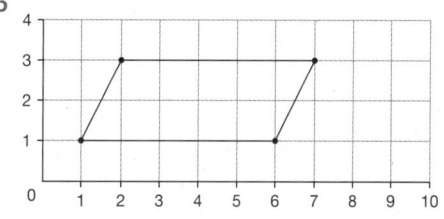

Parallelogram (accept quadrilateral)

16 A **(2,4)** B **(6,2)** C **(10,8)** D **(12,6)**
17 a–b

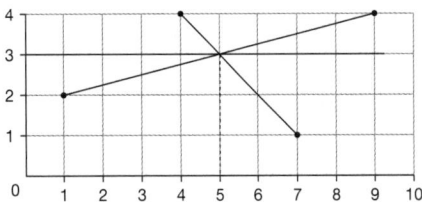

   c **(5,3)**
   d E.g. **(2,3) and (4,3)** (accept any coordinates where the y value (the second number) is 3)
18 **96** 1 kg = 1000 g so 2 kg = 2000 g and 500 × 4 = 2000 g; 24 × 4 = 96
19 a **20 days** 200 divided by 10 = 20
    b **30 g** 5 g × 2 × 3 = 30 g
20 **87½ cm** A pentagon has 5 sides so multiply by 5: 17 × 5 = 85 and 5 lots of ½ = 2½; 85 + 2½ = 87½
21 a **215 m** 860 ÷ 4 = 215 m
    b **2580 m** 860 × 3 = 2580 m
22 **4 packs** 8 m × 3 m = 24 sq m, 24 ÷ 6 = 4
23 **09:05 09:17 09:29 09:41 09:53**
24 a **10 km**
    b **10.30**
    c **15 km**
25 **£23.50** Savings are £4.25 × 6 = £25.50, £25.50 – £2.25 = £23.25
26 **13 minutes** Arrive at station at 9.25, got on bus 32 minutes before 9.25, which is 8.53, 8.53 – 8.40 = 13 minutes
27 a **£49.50** 20 at £2.75 = £55, 2 at £2.75 = £5.50, £55 – £5.50 = £49.50
    b **£5.50**
28 **7524**
29 **£1506.50** £6026 ÷ 4 = £1506.50
30 **24** 360 ÷ 5 = 72, 72 ÷ 3 = 24
31 **82.63** 52.58 + 30.05 = 82.63
32 a **5** 3057 ÷ 100 = 30.5̲7
    b **0** 8204 × 100 = 82̲0 400

Mixed Paper 4

1 a **34** 6 × 12 = 72, 72 – 4 = 68, 68 – 34 = 34
   b **4154**

4	8	9	11 2	12
	7		6	8
4	1		5	4

   c **48** 96 ÷ 4 = 24, 24 × 2 = 48
2 b There is a repeating pattern of three shapes: large circle – small circle – square, with an arrow pointing out rotating anticlockwise by half a right angle each time.
3 c The V shape has one straight line rotating clockwise as if around the edges of a square, and a black spot moves along the diagonal line repeating the pattern of end – middle – corner position on that line.
4 d The number of lines in the zigzag increase by one, and the short line moves down the zigzags in successive shapes.
5 e The number of circles in the chain increases by one each time, alternately adding a black and then a white circle, and the lines on the top circle alternate between plain lines and arrows.
6 e All of the shapes on the left are squares with a diagonal line across them and a curved line going from the centre of that line to one outer corner and extending beyond it, with a black triangle on the outer opposite corner of the square.
7 e All of the shapes on the left have an outer dotted line and an inner plain line, with a single line circle in the middle.
8 c All of the patterns on the left have 6 elements.
9 d All of the shapes on the left have half shaded and one small shape in the unshaded half.
10

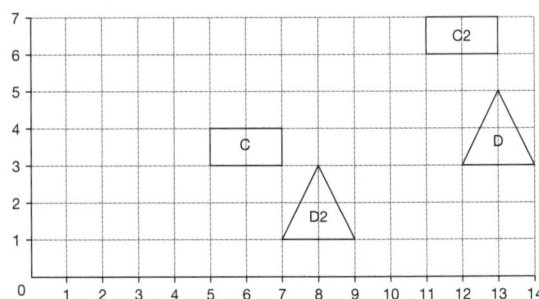

11 a **12**
    b **1080 degrees** 360 × 3 = 1080 degrees
12 Obtuse angles must be more than 90 degrees and less than 180 degrees.
13 **180 degrees** Minute hand moves from pointing at the 12 to the 6, which is 180 degrees.
14 **Right 4, up 4**
15 **Right 9, down 4**
16 and 17

18 **10 cm** 640 ÷ 8 = 80, 80 ÷ 8 = 10
19 **280** 70 × 50 × 80 cm cubes or 7 × 5 × 8 10 cm cubes, which is 35 × 8 = 280
20 **493 litres** 4 weeks = 28 days, 4 days is 250 × 4 = 1000 ml = 1 litre, 28 ÷ 4 = 7, 500 litres – 7 litres = 493 litres
21 **34 million** 1000 litres × 1000 = 1 000 000 ml, so 34 000 000 ml
22 a **27**
    b **13** 25 – 12 = 13
23 a **6**
    b **⅓** 5 out of 15 only have dogs, which gives $\frac{5}{15}$; divide both numbers by 5 to simplify to $\frac{1}{3}$
24 $\frac{4}{14}$ $\frac{5}{20}$ $\frac{6}{18}$ $\frac{7}{28}$ $\frac{4}{10}$ $\frac{3}{12}$
25 **47** ½ of 52 = 26 and 63 ÷ 3 = 21; 26 + 21 = 47

26 a **A £250, B £125, C £100**
500 ÷ 2 = 250; 500 ÷ 4 = 125;
b **£25** 250 + 125 + 100 = 475, 500 − 475 = 25
27 To change analogue time to 24-hour clock, add 12 to the hours between 1 p.m. and 11 p.m. To change 24hr-clock into analogue time, subtract 12 from the hours after 13:00. Make sure 4 digits are shown (in the hours before 10 a zero is inserted at the beginning, e.g. 09:00, 08:00, and so on).

A.m. or p.m. times	24-hour clock	Time written in words
3.00 a.m.	03:00	Three o'clock in the morning
10.15 a.m.	10:15	Quarter past ten in the morning
4.25 p.m.	16:25	Twenty-five past four in the afternoon (accept evening)
11.30 p.m.	23:30	Half past eleven at night

28 a **10.30 a.m.** 9 a.m. + 45 mins = 9.45, 9.45 + 45 mins = 10.30
b **12.20 p.m.** 10.30 + 20 mins = 10.50, 10.50 + 45 mins = 11.35, 11.35 + 45 mins = 12.20
29 **2400** 1 minute = 60 seconds; 4 x 60 = 240 so 40 x 60 = 2400
30 **20:15** Total delay is 45 + 30 mins = 1 hour 15 mins; should arrive at 13:00 + 6 hours = 19:00, 19:00 + 1 hour 15 min delay = 20:15

Curveball Questions 2

1

2

3 Walkers = 2 hrs as it takes 1 hr to complete 5 km; cyclists = 24 minutes as 25 km per hour ÷ 5 = 5 minutes and 60 minutes ÷ 5 = 12 so 2 x 12 = 24; car = 15 minutes as 40 ÷ 4 = 10 km and 60 minutes ÷ 4 = 15 minutes.
a **Walkers leave at 11 a.m., cyclists at 12.36 p.m., car at 12.45 p.m.**
b **3.24 p.m.**

Test Paper 1

1 a **15** 48_6_0.37
b **9** 5_2_0.041
2 a **3** 74_5_0.25 5 − 2 = 3
b **7** 732_1_.93 9 − 2 = 7
3 **7 301 024.9**
4 **48, 6, 2, 136** 42 + 6 = 48; 48 ÷ 8 = 6; 6 − 4 = 2; 2 + 134 = 136
5 **141** 500 − 359 = 141
6 a **16, 19** The difference between each number is 3 and the numbers get bigger so it is added (13 + 3 = 16 and 16 + 3 = 19)
b **39, 33** The difference is is 6 and the numbers get smaller so it is subtracted (45 − 6 = 39 and 39 − 6 = 33)
7 **145, 190** The difference is is 15 and the numbers get bigger so it is added (130 + 15 = 145 and 175 + 15 = 190)
8 **50** Half of 400 = 200, quarter of 200 is 50.
9 $\frac{4}{8} = \frac{6}{12} = \frac{5}{10} = \frac{7}{14} = \frac{50}{100}$. All fractions are equivalents of $\frac{1}{2}$
10 **c** All of the shapes on the left have diagonal line shading and one black circle inside the shape.
11 **e** All of the shapes on the left are squares with a circle across one edge and a single-headed arrow going in and out of the square.
12 **d** All of the shapes on the left have five lines with a crossing point between two of the lines.
13 **d** All of the shapes on the left have five sides, an inner plain line and an outer dashed line.
14 **d**
15 **e**
16 **c**
17 **b**
18 **d** All of the shapes except d are triangles with one smaller black shape within them.
19 **a** All of the shapes except a are made up of three loops with a dot in the central loop.
20 **b** All of the shapes except b are made up of five lines.
21 **d** All of the shapes except d have arrowheads with the same shading at each end.
22 **c** The number of lines in the first square give the number of sides for the shape in the second square.
23 **d** The number of horizontal lines in the first pattern give the number of horizontal lines pointing right at the top of the line in the second pattern.
24 **e** The shading of the loop in the first shape becomes the shading of the other loop in the second shape.
25 **b** The first shape is rotated 90 degrees clockwise to give the second shape.
26 **44 mins** Advertisements last 3 x 2 = 6 mins; 6.30 to 7.20 is 50 mins; 50 mins − 6 mins = 44 mins
27 **21°C** A is 8° warmer than C, so A is 15°; A is 6° cooler than B, so B is 21°.
28 a **32 biscuits** Chocolate biscuits are $\frac{1}{4}$, so total is 8 x 4 = 32
b **8 plain biscuits** Number of plain biscuits is 32 − 10 creams − 8 chocolate − 6 ginger = 8
29 a **4**
b **8**
c **12**
d **2**

30 a **Octagon**
   b **Kite**
   c **Pentagon**
   d **Trapezium**
31 a Any four-sided shape with four different length sides.
   b Any triangle with three sides of different lengths.
   c Any six-sided shape with different length sides.
32 a **b and f** have an X as they are obtuse angles.
   b **c** has a square in the right angle.
33 a **A (1,7) B (3,8) C (5,5) D (2,5)**
   b **X (2,2) Y (8,1) Z (11,3)**
   c
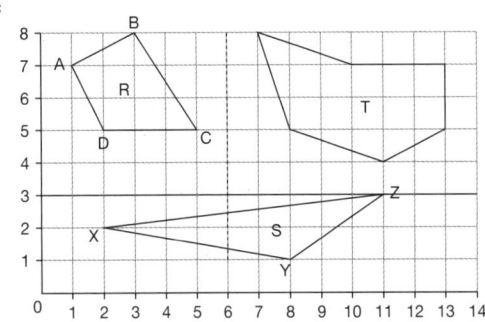
   d **R a quadrilateral   S a (scalene) triangle   T a hexagon**
34 **(6,3)**
35 **68** $8 \times 8 = 64, \frac{1}{2} \times 8 = 4, 64 + 4 = 68$
36 **20 m** $50 \times 2 = 100, 140 - 100 = 40, 40 \div 2 = 20$
37 a **24 000 cubic cm**
      $20 \times 30 \times 40 = 600 \times 40 = 24\,000$
   b **18 000 cubic cm**
      $20 \times 30 \times 30 = 600 \times 30 = 18\,000$
   c **6000** $24\,000 - 18\,000 = 6000$
38 1 litre = 1000 ml, so multiply by 1000
   a **64 000 ml**
   b **3750 ml**
   c **100 000 ml**
39 a **1000 cubic mm** 10 mm = 1 cm, so 10 × 10 × 10 = 1000
   b **1 000 000 cubic cm** 100 cm in 1 m, so 100 × 100 × 100 = 1 000 000
40 **1 hour 10 mins** 11:30 – 10:20 = 1 hour 10 mins
41 **20 mins** A to D on the 3rd train is 11:30 to 12:15 = 45 mins; on the 4th train it is 12:40 to 13:45 = 1 hour 5 mins, 1 hour 5 mins – 45 mins = 20 mins
42 **1st train and 4th train** 9:10–10:15 is 1 hour 5 mins, 12:40–13:45 is 1 hour 5 mins.
43 **5 mins** 13:05 to 13:20 is 15 mins, 14:20 to 14:40 is 20 mins, the difference is 20 – 15 = 5 mins
44 a **21 children**
   b **2** 4 – 2 = 2
   c **green orange yellow purple red blue**
45 a **20 cars**
   b **10** 14 – 4 = 10
   c **lorries   bikes**
46 a **30 children**
   b $\frac{3}{20}$ or $\frac{15}{100}$ 17 × 5 = 85 and 100 – 85 = 15; $\frac{15}{100}$ can be simplified to $\frac{3}{20}$
   c **10 children** $\frac{1}{2}$ of 20 = 10

47 a **32**
   b **4** 8 – 4 = 4
   c **10** strawberry + chocolate = 8 + 10 = 18, mint + lemon = 4 + 4 = 8, 18 – 8 = 10
48 a **59** 24 + 35 = 59
   b **54** 24 + 30 = 54
   c **13** 24 – 11 = 13
49

	Plays hockey	Does not play hockey
Plays table tennis	10	8
Does not play table tennis	10	4

50 **£62.11** £372.66 ÷ 6 = £62.11
51 **1541.25** 308.25 × 5 = 1541.25

Test Paper 2

1 **2253.1**
2 **4661**

```
4 -5  9 10  13 4  10
         3    7    9
      ─────────────
      4  6    6    1
```

3 **b** The upside down L-shape alternates between facing left and facing right, the shading of the small square follows a repeating pattern of white, black, a cross.
4 **e** The number of black circles on the line increases by one each time, and there is a white circle at the end in each pattern.
5 **d** The black circle moves from lower left to the centre to the top left in successive squares then repeats the pattern, an there is a white circle in the top left corner in alternate squares.
6 **d** The diagonal lines off the main line decrease by one each time, first decreasing by one on the right side and then by one on the left side, and the number of short lines projecting from the circle increase by one each time.
7 **e** The first letter represents the position of the triangle on the square (A at the bottom, B at the top, C at the side); the second letter represents the shading of the square (X is horizontal lines, Y is diagonal lines, Z is vertical lines).
8 **b** The first letter represents the shape inside the square (A is a circle, B is a triangle, C is a square); the second letter represents the side of the straight line below the square (X is on the left, Y is on the right).
9 **d** The first letter represents the number of horizontal lines (D is 3, E is 2, F is 1); the second letter represents the number of vertical lines (X is 1, Y is 2, Z is 3).
10 **b** The first letter represents the circle style (A is large with an inner dotted line, B is large with two plain lines, C is small with two plain lines, D is small with an inner dotted line); the second letter represents the central shape (X is a plain black spot, Y is a black spot with one line through it, Z is a black spot with two lines through it).

11 **d** The first letter represents the shading of the shape below the triangle (L has vertical lines, M is white, N is black); the second letter represents the orientation of the triangle (R has the right angle in the lower right, S has the right angle in the lower left, T has the right angle at the top).

12 **e** The first letter represents the position of the black bar across the rectangle (A is at the top, B is in the middle, C is at the bottom); the second letter represents the number of spots (X is 4, Y is 3, Z is 2).

13 **c** The first letter represents the number of sides of the larger shape (D has 6, E has 5, F has 4); the second letter represents the position of the circle (R is outside the larger shape, S is across the line, T is inside the shape).

14 **d**

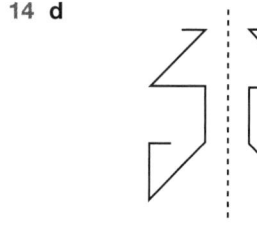

15 **c**

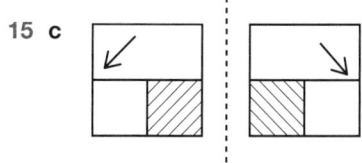

16 **e**

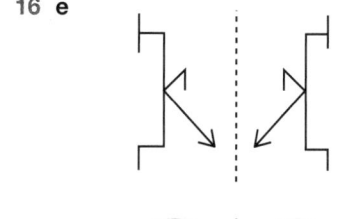

17 **b**

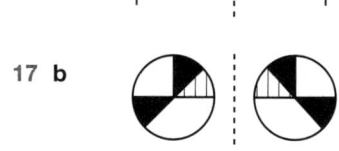

18 **8104.6** 405.23 × 10 = 4052.3, 4052.3 × 2 = 804.6
19 **0.5, 0.3, 0.75**
20 **24.91**

```
  4 11 ²9 ¹⁰ . 1 6   8
  3  9  5  .  7   7
  ─────────────────────
           2  4  .  9   1
```

21 **97.95**

```
    3 5 . 7
    5 1 . 3 8
    1 0 . 8 7
  ─────────────
    9 7 . 9 5
        1   1
```

22 **£86.05** £84.55 + 85p + 65p = £84.55 + £1.50 = £86.05

23 **Dan** Order according to the information given:
Tallest ? Dan James ? Dan Ralph ? Dan Tom Shortest
We know James is taller than Ralph and Tom, and if James is second tallest, then only Dan can be taller than James.

24 **24 eggs** dozen = 12 and 12 × 20 = 240; 240 ÷ 10 = 24
$\frac{1}{10} \times 240 = 24$

25 **a** trapezium **b** isosceles triangle **c** kite

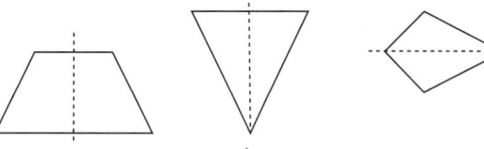

26 **a** quadrilateral
b *either* **rectangle** and **four** *or* **square** and **four**
c *either* **equilateral** and **three** *or* **isosceles** and **two**

27 **a** triangular prism
b square-based pyramid
c cylinder
d cube

28

29 **90°** There are 12 numbers on a clock face so divided 360° by 12 (360 ÷ 12 = 30); from 2 o'clock to 5 o'clock will be 3 lots of 30° and 3 × 30 = 90

30 **a** right 4, down 3
b left 9, up 4
c and **d**

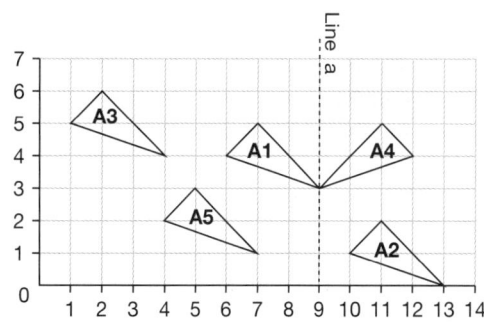

e **(4,2) (5,3) (7,1)** in any order

31 **10 kg** 22 lbs is 2.2 × 10, so 1 kg × 10 = 10 kg
32 **3 km 407 m 58 cm** 3407.58 m 1000 m = 1 km, so 3000, = 3 km, 100 cm = 1 m, so 0.58 m = 58 cm
33 **5400 secs** 1 hour = 60 mins, $\frac{1}{2}$ hour = 30 mins, 90 mins = 90 × 60 secs = 5400 secs
34 **248 mm** 1 cm = 10 mm and 1240 cm × 10 = 1240 mm; 1240 ÷ 5 = 248
35 Count the number of whole squares.
Remember two 1/2 squares = 1 whole square.
a **7 sq cm**
b **8 sq cm**
c **8 sq cm**
d **6 sq cm**

36 a **26 cm** 34 × 2 = 68, 120 − 68 = 52, $\frac{1}{2}$ of 52 = 26
   b **1054 sq cm** 31 × 34 is 34 × 10 = 340,
   340 × 3 = 1020, 1020 + 34 = 1054
37 a **7**
   b **08:02, 08:11, 08:20, 08:29, 08:38, 08:47, 08:56**
   c **09:05**
38 a **8.32 a.m.** 8.55 − 23mins = 8.32
   b **8.17 a.m.** 8.32 − 15 mins = 8.17
   c **6 hours 35 mins** 8.55 − 9 a.m. is 5 mins,
   9 a.m. to 3.30 p.m. is $6\frac{1}{2}$ hours so the total is
   6 hours 35 mins.
39 a **10 seconds**
   b **80 degrees**
   c **35 seconds**
40 a **8**
   b **21**
   c **4**
   d **28** 21 + 4 + 3 = 28
   e **7**
   f **carrots** Carrots: 12 + 21 + 7 + 4 = 44
   Peas: 21 + 8 + 7 + 3 = 39
   Tomatoes: 7 + 3 + 4 + 5 = 19
41 a **20** 12 + 8 = 20
   b **16**
   c **8** 32 − 24 = 8
   d $\frac{3}{4}$ 24/32 = $\frac{3}{4}$
42 **c** All of the shapes except c have one black circle inside the shape and one outside it.
43 **d** All of the shapes except d are made up of a circle, a triangle and a square.
44 **b** All of the patterns except b have the overlapping section of the two shapes shaded black.
45 a **28, 4, 20** 36 − 8   28 ÷ 7   4 × 5   20
   b **15, 125, 25** 5 × 3   15 + 110   125 ÷ 5   25
46 a **72** 30 + 6 = 36, 36 × 2 = 72
   b **79** 30 × 3 = 90, 90 − 11 = 79
47 a **6 units**
   b **6 thousands** (accept 6000)
   c **6 tenths** (accept $\frac{6}{10}$)
   d **6 hundreds** (accept 600)
48 a **85, 81**
   101 97 93 89 89 − 4 = 85 85 − 4 = 81
     −4 −4 −4 −4 −4   −4
   b **20, 25**
   10 11 13 16 16 + 4 = 20 20 + 5 = 25
     +1 +2 +3   +4   +5
49 a **4** 14 − 10 = 4
   b **11** 16 − 5 = 11
   c **27** 18 + 9 = 27
   d **72** 10 + 14 + 5 + 16 + 18 + 9 = 72

Notes

Notes

Progress Chart

Learning Papers

Number Skills /28

Sequences /24

Number Skills and Pattern Recognition /32

Logic and Codes /28

Shape, Space and Grids /27

Position and Direction /33

Measurement and Pairs /35

Statistics and Pattern Recognition /32

Curveball Questions 1 /15

Curveball Questions 2 /20

Mixed Papers

	1	2	3	4
1				
2				
3				
4				
5				
6				
7				
8				
9				
10				
11				
12				
13				
14				
15				
16				
17				
18				
19				
20				
21				
22				
23				
24				
25				
26				
27				
28				
29				
30				
31				
32				
33				
34				
35				
36				
37				
38				
39				
40				
	/40	/40	/40	/40

Test Papers

Test Paper 1 /75

Test Paper 1 /70